Perils
of Power

OTHER BOOKS BY RICHARD EXLEY

The Rhythm of Life

The Painted Parable

The Other God —
Seeing God As He Really Is

Perils
of Power

by

RICHARD EXLEY

A Division of Harrison House, Inc.
Tulsa, Oklahoma

Unless otherwise indicated, all Scripture quotations
are taken from *The Holy Bible: New International
Version,* copyright © 1978 by the International Bible
Society. Used by permission of Zondervan Bible Publishers.

Scriptures marked KJV are taken from the *King James
Version* of the Bible.

Cover photo: Scott Miller

Perils of Power
ISBN 0-89274-525-8
Copyright © 1988 by Richard Exley
7807 E. 76th St.
Tulsa, Oklahoma 74133-3678

Published by Honor Books
A Division of Harrison House, Inc.
P. O. Box 35035
Tulsa, Oklahoma 74153

CONTENTS

PREFACE

To speak or write prophetically is risky at best, even in good times, but to hear from God, to be charged by Him to address the evils of our present perilous times is more than most men will submit to, for the task is awesome.

I have known Pastor Richard Exley to move under the Lord's Spirit-filled anointing in a prophetic way. He has searched his own heart and soul first, always. Perhaps this is why God has now chosen him to address ministers, yes, even all of Christendom, in clear, uncompromising terms that direct us to repentance and restoration. Even better, it reveals how to safeguard all ministers from future failure. In "Perils of Power," God has released through Pastor Exley wisdom beyond man's own knowledge.

E. H. Jim Ammerman, Th.D., D.D.

Chaplain, Colonel
U.S. Army, Retired

President and Director of Chaplaincy
Full-Gospel Churches

INTRODUCTION

If you are older than thirty-five, you can undoubtedly remember where you were and what you were doing that tragic November afternoon in 1963 when President John F. Kennedy was shot. I was sitting on the steps, between classes, at South Houston High School when a girl came running down the hall weeping.

"The President has been shot," she sobbed and ran on.

Her words left me dazed and stunned, with that historic moment forever etched on my mind.

Nor will I ever forget the moment I learned of the Jimmy Swaggart tragedy. A squall of disjointed emotions swept over me — disbelief, shame, anger, grief. All night I tossed and turned, tormented by a host of unholy dreams in which this, the latest in a series of moral tragedies, was replayed again and again. My grief bordered on depression. I grieved for Jimmy Swaggart and his family. I grieved for the ministry around the world. I grieved for the Body of Christ, for the man and woman in the pew; their pain became my pain.

The next few days were hardly better. Each day seemed to bring another disconcerting disclosure — Assemblies of

God officials had been given photos of Jimmy Swaggart entering and leaving a motel with a known prostitute. *Christianity Today* (Mar. 18, 1988) reported, "One denominational official present at the closed meeting described Swaggart's sin as 'sexual misconduct over a period of years.' " *Newsweek* (Mar. 7, 1988) wrote, "Swaggart's secret sin, as some told it, was cruising the sleazy motels along New Orleans' Airline Highway, soliciting prostitutes to strip for him and perform various sexual acts." Swaggart himself made a detailed confession to Assemblies of God officials and a public confession (although not to specific sins) to the congregation of The Family Worship Center in Baton Rouge, Louisiana.

Watching the telecast of that service, I couldn't help but be touched by his tearful confession and by the congregation's obvious compassion. Surely the Lord was proud of their unconditional love. Truly it was both a holy moment and a tragic one.

Yet, as powerful as that moment was, I couldn't help but feel that God was requiring something more of us than unconditional love and forgiveness. Not less than that but more! Jimmy Swaggart had sinned, to be sure, and he will answer to God, but this was more than one man's sin. In a larger sense his transgression indicts the Church as a whole and demands that we re-examine the way we do ministry. Perhaps the fatal flaw is not to be found in the man alone but in the whole Body of Christ. He is, after all, not the first nationally known minister to sin sexually, but simply the latest in an ever-growing list.

According to a recent article in *Leadership* (Winter 1988), local pastors too struggle with sexual temptation, and a significant percentage of them have succumbed. Of the

300 pastors who responded to a confidential survey conducted by the research department of *Christianity Today*, 23 percent said that since they had been in the local church ministry they had done something with someone (not their spouse) that they felt was sexually inappropriate. Twelve percent acknowledged that they had had sexual intercourse with someone other than their spouse, and 18 percent admitted that they had participated in other forms of sexual contact with someone other than their spouse, i.e. passionate kissing, fondling/mutual masturbation. Of this total only 4 percent said they were found out.

The problem then, it seems, is church-wide and underlines the fact that ministers are human beings with the same ego needs and sexual drives as other men — with one significant difference. Other men can acknowledge their humanity, their propensity for sin, and receive the counsel and support of the Church. For the most part, the minister must live in denial. He has no one to turn to. He is afraid to go to a counselor or fellow pastor for fear that word of his problems might somehow leak out. Or as one minister wrote, "I wouldn't dare tell a fellow minister my problems in this area. My denomination would forgive murder, but not impurity of thought."[1] That's probably slightly overstated, but he does have a point, and the resulting isolation leaves the minister terribly vulnerable.

Immorality in the ministry is not a new problem; it is not unique to our age. Tom Schaefer, staff writer for the *Wichita Eagle Beacon,* writes, "Over the years, sexual indiscretion and misconduct have scarred many clergy — as well as those involved with them. From medieval popes who fathered children in violation of their vows of celibacy, to American evangelists who caused scandals by their philandering, to priests whose pedophilia prompted huge payments to settle lawsuits against the church — sexual misconduct by clergy has had an unholy history."[2]

The question I hear most often is, "How could he do something like that?" Perhaps because the issue is so painful, or because it is so fraught with emotion, the questions are seldom, if ever, really answered. And therein lies a second tragedy — we fail to learn from our mistakes and, failing to learn, we are doomed to repeat them. The purpose of *Perils of Power* then, is to consider the "whys" and the "hows" in an effort to understand the interpersonal dynamics of moral failure among those who recognize it as a deadly sin. And, once apprised of these spiritual and emotional dynamics, to effect a preventative strategy.

Moral failure in the ministry, as you've probably already concluded, is a complex issue involving a variety of causes. In the case of Jimmy Swaggart, it appears to be the consummation of a lifelong battle with pornography. If the news reports are accurate, he was driven by lust to seek sexual pleasure with a prostitute. And herein lies the ultimate danger of pornography — it never satisfies, it almost always leads to something more. As one recovering minister wrote of his experiences with pornography, "A magazine excites, a movie thrills, a live show really makes the blood run. I never got as far as body tattooing, personal photograph sessions, and massages, let alone outright prostitution, but I've experienced enough of the unquenchable nature of sex to frighten me for good. Lust does not satisfy; it stirs up."[3]

All sexual sin, however, is not rooted in lust — at least not initially. When a local pastor commits adultery it is usually with someone with whom he has developed a relationship. It is good gone awry. Sexual temptation for him is often rooted, not in vice, but in virtue. What began as legitimate ministry — a shared project perhaps, compassionate listening, the giving of comfort — becomes an emotional bonding, which ultimately leads to an illicit affair. The minister who does a great deal of counseling, or who spends an extended amount of time with a member of the opposite sex, usually in church-related projects, is especially vulnerable to this kind of temptation.

While sexual sin can strike at any time, it is no coincidence that many a minister has succumbed to the tender trap during mid-life, at the height of his career. Having achieved more success than he ever dreamed possible, he reaches mid-life only to discover that, for all his achievements, he is still unfulfilled. During this period of disillusionment he is especially susceptible to the affirmation of the opposite sex. It feels good to be appreciated as a man and not just a minister. He has no intention of committing adultery. But as Dr. Carlfred Broderick notes, after working with numerous couples who were fully committed to fidelity yet who found themselves involved in an adulterous relationship, ". . . With a little help from rationalization, the sympathy leads smoothly into tenderness, the tenderness to the need for privacy, the privacy to physical consolation, and the consolation straight to bed."[4]

And, finally, there are those who have become victims of their own success. They are powerful men surrounded by "yes men." No one really holds them accountable, and over a period of time they are able to justify almost any desire they have. The laws of God which apply to ordinary people are amended to suit their lifestyles. One thing leads to another until even infidelity can be rationalized.

Without question we are experiencing a moral crisis in the ministry, but moral failure need not be inevitable. Victory, however, does not lie in denying our humanity. Repression does not work. Our sexual drives, our belonging needs, and even our ambitions are an intrinsic part of who we are. Destroy them and we destroy a part of ourselves. Repress them and they will eventually manifest themselves, usually, in inappropriate and unacceptable ways. Our only hope is to surrender our humanity to God, allow Him to redeem it; that is, channel it into appropriate areas of fulfillment. We can live a victorious life, but in order to do so we must accept the Lordship of Jesus Christ, live and minister under accountability, and establish appropriate guidelines before we have become so emotionally involved that rational thinking has been replaced by passionate rationalization.

Footnotes

[1]"How Common is Pastoral Indiscretion?" *Leadership* (Winter Quarter, 1988), p. 13.

[2]Tom Schaefer, "Sex and the Clergy," *Wichita Eagle Beacon* (Mar. 5, 1988, Sect. E), pp. 1,2.

[3]Name Withheld, "The War Within: An Anatomy of Lust," *Leadership* (Fall Quarter, 1982), p. 34.

[4]Carlfred Broderick, *Couples* (New York: Simon and Schuster, Inc., 1979), p. 163.

Chapter 1

LUST: THE WAR WITHIN

"I am writing this article anonymously because I am embarrassed. Embarrassed for my wife and children, yes, but embarrassed most for myself."

So begins an article in *Leadership* (Fall 1982), written by an anonymous minister, in which he details his personal struggle with lust. He continues:

". . . if I believed I were the only one who fought in that war, I would not waste emotional energy dredging up stained and painful memories. But I believe my experience is not uncommon, is perhaps even typical of *pastors, writers,* and *conference speakers.* No one talks about it. No one writes about it. But it's there, like an unacknowledged cancer that metastasizes best when no one goes for x-rays or feels for lumps.

"I know I am not alone, because the few times I have opened up and shared my struggles with Christian friends, they have replied with Doppelganger stories of exactly the same stage of awakening, obsession, possession . . . ."[1] (emphasis mine)

I first read that article almost six years ago and I must admit that, while I did not doubt the reality of the writer's personal struggle, I certainly couldn't concur with his conclusions concerning its prevalence in the ministry. However, events in the ensuing five years, especially the last twelve to eighteen months, have forced me to re-examine my thinking.

First there was the man, a spiritual leader in his own church, who came to my office for counseling: "He chose to see me rather than his own pastor, so great was his shame. He had done a despicable thing, and now he couldn't live with himself. Hardly had I closed the office door before he fell to his knees sobbing. For several minutes he wept before the Lord. Finally he was able to compose himself and only then did he share his dark secret.

"It had started innocently enough with morning coffee at a nearby convenience store. Then he started browsing through the pornographic magazines on the counter while he drank his coffee. Then he purchased one, then another.

"From that point, the story has an all too familiar progression. From magazines he went to x-rated videos, and then he secured the services of a prostitute. Of course, this degenerating progression didn't happen overnight. It took place over a period of months and with each step he told himself he would go no farther, but he seemed powerless to stop.

"He lived in a self-made hell. There were moments of lustful pleasure, to be sure, but they were followed by hours of shame, days and weeks of unspeakable regret. Yet even in his shame he was irresistibly drawn toward the very thing he hated. His desperate prayers seemed powerless against the demons within. Now he lived in secrecy and fear. What if someone saw him? What if his wife or someone from his church found out? His marriage suffered, as did his church life. He wanted out, he wanted to stop, but something seemed to drive him on.

"Then his worst fears were realized. He contracted a sexually transmitted disease and infected his wife with it. Thankfully it wasn't AIDS, but it still meant that he had to tell her so she could receive treatment. What was going to happen now? Would she forgive him? Could she ever trust him again? How foolish, how insane, his sins now seemed."[2]

Next came the PTL debacle with its disconcerting revelation of excesses — financially as well as sexually. Not to mention the sinful fall of several prominent but less well-known ministers. Some of them were just names to me, but from time to time it struck closer to home.

I remember one pastor who confessed to a sexual affair with a member of his congregation. That was tragic enough, but shortly thereafter he was accused of renting and viewing x-rated videos. When confronted with irrefutable evidence, he acknowledged that he had indeed rented them, but only to collect evidence to use in a campaign to rid his city of pornography. Perhaps his explanation is legitimate, I certainly hope so, but in any case it was just another incident in an ever-unfolding series of events which have forced me to reconsider the prevalence of lust among ministers.

And finally there was the Jimmy Swaggart tragedy.

It allegedly grew out of a lifelong battle with pornography which ultimately led to a meeting with a New Orleans prostitute who performed pornographic acts for him but did not have intercourse with him. Given the

17

spiritual climate following the Bakker debacle, Gorman's threats, and what Swaggart stood to lose, one cannot doubt the terrible hold it had on him. Even if a denominational official, present at the closed meeting with Swaggart, had not described his sin as "sexual misconduct over a period of years,"[3] any thinking person would have come to the same conclusions. No minister, especially one of Jimmy Swaggart's stature, suddenly decides to visit a prostitute. It's the tragic consummation of a long and undoubtedly lonely battle against the enemy within — lust.

The point of all of this is not to discredit the ministry, or to inflict any further pain on those who have succumbed to the mesmerizing power of lust, but to bring to light the deadly war within. I cannot help but wonder how many ministers might have been spared the tragedy of moral failure if only they had had someone to go to when temptation first reared its ugly head. Unfortunately, temptation which is allowed to grow in secret soon infects the whole person, distorting his values and undermining his resistance. Remember, Satan is patient. He doesn't mind waiting half a lifetime if in the end he can bring a spiritual leader crashing down.

The power of such temptation is rooted in its secrecy. It flourishes in the dark, behind closed doors, denied and unacknowledged, except for those terrifying times when it exacts its terrible toll. Then it leaves its victim shamed and guilt-ridden, determined that it will never happen again, but still locked in his debilitating silence.

Just before his sin was made public Jimmy Swaggart wrote: "I have always taken pride in my spiritual strength. I have believed that in my relationship with God, if He promised me something, I could have it. I can't recall, in all of my life, ever going to anybody and asking them for help."[4] In his televised confession, before the congregation of The Family Worship Center in Baton Rouge, he said something to the effect that he had never really allowed himself to be just another man. He continued: "I have always believed with God's help I could do anything. Now I realize that if I had turned to my brothers and sisters I surely would have found the help I needed to win the victory over this." (paraphrased)

It would appear that he has belatedly realized that sexual sins can seldom be overcome without the support of a spiritual brother or mentor, especially a "private" sin like pornography. In truth, until it is confessed to another person, as well as to God, it keeps us in bondage. (See James 5:16.) Yet, what minister will dare risk such a confession when to do so is to have his sin made known to his wife, his brethren, and quite possibly his church. Instead he struggles in secret with both his failure and his ever-increasing guilt.

And the more successful a man becomes, the harder it is for him to risk such a confession. He has too much to lose, too many people will be hurt. Even his success becomes part of the trap. He has a reputation to maintain, an image to protect; only that's all it is — an image. In truth he is a tormented man, fighting a lonely and losing battle against the sinful habits of a lifetime. He is not a bad man, not a hypocrite. He hates himself for what he has become — a public minister, a man of God, with a secret life. If the truth were known, he has probably spent many a night in desperate prayer only to succumb again. He really does love the Lord and the Lord's work, but he doesn't know how to make it work for himself.

19

And if his secret addiction is not overcome it will destroy him, not immediately, but eventually. A man may be losing the battle within even as he experiences success in the ministry. But do not be deceived; in the end, sin will exact its just due.

The unnamed writer of the aforementioned *Leadership* article shares a tragic account which is a case in point:

"Exactly three days later I spent the night with a very dear friend, a pastor of one of the largest churches in the South. I had never shared intimate details of my lust life with anyone before, but the schizophrenia was building to such a point I felt I must. He listened quietly, with compassion and great sensitivity as I recounted a few incidents, skipping over those that showed me in the worst light, and described some of my fears to him.

"He sat for a long time with sad eyes after I had finished speaking. We both watched our freshly refilled cups of coffee steam, then stop steaming, then grow cold. I waited for his words of advice or comfort or healing or something. I needed a priest at that moment, someone to say, 'Your sins are forgiven.'

"But my friend was no priest. He did something I never expected. His lip quivered at first, the skin on his face began twitching, and finally he started sobbing — great, huge, wretched sobs such as I had seen only at funerals.

"In a few moments, when he had recovered some semblance of self-control, I learned the truth. My friend was not sobbing for me; he was sobbing for himself. He began to tell me of his own expedition into lust. He had been where I was — five years before. Since that time, he had taken lust to its logical consequences. I will not dwell on sordid details, but my friend had tried it all: bondage, prostitution, bi-sexualism, orgies. He reached inside his vest pocket and pulled out a pad of paper showing the prescriptions he took to fight the venereal disease and anal infections he had picked up along the way. He carries the pad with him on trips, he explained, to buy the drugs in cities where he is anonymous.

"I saw my friend dozens of times after that and learned every horrific detail of his hellish life. I worried about cognitive dissonance; he brooded on suicide. I read about deviance; he performed it. I winced at subtle fissures in my marriage; he was in divorce litigation.

". . . If I had learned about my friend's journey to debauchery in an article like this one, I doubtless would have clucked my tongue, questioned LEADERSHIP'S judgement in printing it, and rejected the author as an insincere poseur in the faith. But I knew this man, I thought, as well as I knew anyone. His insights, compassion, and love were all more mature than mine. My sermons were like freshman practice runs compared to his. He was a godly man if I had ever met one, but underneath all that . . . my inner fear jumped uncontrollably. I sensed the power of evil."[5]

Imagine, if you can, how different the outcome might be if early on the struggling minister had been able to confess his temptation, even his sin, to a trusted mentor without fear of exposure or recrimination. Voluntarily he could have submitted himself to confidential rehabilitation. Under the godly counsel of those in authority he could have been fully restored to effective ministry. If, on the other hand, such actions had failed to rehabilitate him, then public disciplinary action could have been taken. If indeed the goal of church discipline is redemptive and not punitive, then nothing is gained through public disclosure when the minister voluntarily confesses and seeks help.

There are undoubtedly some charlatans in the ministry, men who have no relationship with God, but, for the most part, I believe the majority of ministers sincerely love the Lord and the ministry they have dedicated their lives to, even those who have become a casualty of the war within. This in no way absolves them from the consequences of their behavior, but it does put things in a different light. They are not enemies to be disposed of, not impostors to be weeded out, but brothers to be restored. Paul addresses this issue when he writes, "Brothers, if someone is caught in a sin, you who are spiritual should restore him gently . . ." (Gal. 6:1).

Diagnosing the problem is relatively simple compared to the task of resolving it. It must be dealt with on at least two fronts — individually and as a body. On an individual basis the minister must accept the responsibility for exercising the spiritual disciplines which will enable him to overcome the habits of a lifetime. It won't be easy. After all he has prayed and fought this battle for years with only the most limited success. His disappointments far out-number his victories, but that does not nullify the truth of the Gospel's redeeming power. We cannot, we must not, allow past failures to define our theology. In the depths of despair, following yet another sinful failure, it would be easy to conclude that, while we can be delivered from the eternal penalty of sin, through Jesus Christ, we cannot escape its present power. The scriptures, however, teach otherwise. The cross provides, not only justification, but redemption and deliverance as well!

The fact of our victory over sin was accomplished when Jesus died on the cross. It becomes a present reality in our lives as we ". . . count . . . (ourselves) . . . dead to sin but alive to God in Christ Jesus" (Rom. 6:11). This is not simply wishful thinking but truth, carefully considered, and documented by the scriptures. When Jesus died, He not only died *for* our sins, but also *as* sin. Paul says, "God made him who had no sin to be sin for us . . ." (2 Cor. 5:21). Therefore when He died, sin died — that is, its stranglehold on the human will was broken; it was rendered powerless. Now the only power sin has in the believer's life is what he gives it.

Dr. G. Earl Guinn relates a personal incident which illustrates this truth well. He writes, "Several years ago while spading in my yard, I inadvertently disturbed a snake that had hibernated for the winter months. He came racing out to do battle with the intruder. Stepping aside, I took aim with the shovel point and severed the snake's head from his body. Even though the body was headless, the serpent writhed on the ground for some time before becoming still in death."[6]

On the cross our sinful nature, the "old self," as it were, was crucified with Christ, that is its head was severed from its body. What we experience when temptation comes is simply the death throes of the old man. In truth, his power has been broken. He has been defeated, although not yet fully destroyed. No longer does he sit enthroned on the seat of power in our lives. Now he is on the outside begging to be restored to his former place of power.

"Some time ago
I dreamed a dream
in which there was only one character — me.

23

Only there were two of me,
twins, if you please,
but not identical.

"The first me was the man I know,
the man I was at the time —
thirty-five years old,
about 5'9" tall
and maybe fifteen pounds overweight.

"The other me was the man
I once wanted to be —
more than six feet tall,
with the kind of body
that only steroids and weights
can produce.

"We were standing on the edge of a cliff
overlooking the sea.
A hundred feet below
the surf beat itself into foamy spray
against a wall of jagged rocks.
The steroid me was holding the other me
high above his head
as if he was going to hurl me to my death
on the rocks far below.

"In my dream the real me,
that is the one I recognized,
attempted to reason with the other me,
that muscle-bound maniac,
but to no avail.
I told him he was throwing his life away.
Why hurl me to my death
when he could use his enormous strength and
agility

to pursue a career as a professional athlete?
He seemed not to hear me
and death was imminent.

"Then I awoke in a cold sweat.
Instantly, it seemed,
I knew that dream
was a warning from God.
The steroid me was my ego, my ambition,
the old man.
So strong was he
that I could not contend with him.
He was immune to
my most desperate and impassioned pleas.
God was my only hope,
and there beside my bed
I prayed that He might crucify this old man,
and He did.
God defeated him, but He did not destroy him.

"He broke his power, but he still lives.
He is no longer the 'strong man,'
holding me captive,
and I am no longer at his mercy.
But He is still to be feared.
Now he's a broken man pleading for my
sympathy.
'A crust of bread,' he cries.
'A helping hand for an old friend,' he pleads,
'Just a few minutes of your time.'
So pathetic does he seem
that I am almost tempted to share my life with
him.

"But then I remember that this is no friend,
he is a deadly enemy,
one who takes his life from me.
With determined deliberateness
I turn my back on him.
By God's grace I will starve
this ego maniac.
I will deny his unholy ambition,
day by day, and thus
reckon him dead!"

At the risk of sounding terribly naive, I want to say again that, as believers, sin has no power over us except what we voluntarily give it. Our "old self" is a broken man pleading for our sympathy. "A crust of bread," he cries, "a helping hand for an old friend." So harmless, so pathetic, does he seem that we are often tempted to share our life with him. When we do, however, we discover that he is almost immediately transformed into the "strong man" again. Experience has taught me that a single "yes" can undo a hundred "noes" and can put me under his tyranny again. Our only hope, then, is to deny him at every turn. Or as Paul writes, "Those who belong to Christ Jesus have crucified their sinful nature with its passions and desires" (Gal. 5:24).

What does all of this "theology" have to do with the war within? Everything! Lust is not the result of an overactive sex drive; it is not a biological phenomenon, not the by-product of our glands. If it were, then it could be satisfied with a sexual experience, like a glass of water quenches our thirst, or a good meal satisfies our appetite; but alas, the more we attempt to appease our lust, the more demanding it becomes. There is simply not enough erotica in the world to satisfy its insatiable appetite.

When we ". . . count . . . (ourselves) . . . dead to sin . . . ." (Rom. 6:11), when we crucify our ". . . sinful nature with its passions and desires . . ." (Gal. 5:24) by denying our lustful obsessions, we are not repressing a legitimate drive; rather we are putting to death an aberration. Lust is to the gift of sex what cancer is to a normal cell. Therefore we deny it, not in order to become sexless saints, but in order to be fully alive to God, which includes the full and uninhibited expression of our sexual being within the God-given context of marriage.

Romans 8:13 states: "For if you live according to the sinful nature, you will die; but if by the Spirit you put to death the misdeeds of the body, you will live . . . ."

We can be delivered from lust, but in truth, lust can only be defeated by a combination of divine deliverance and daily discipline. Without the direct intervention of the Holy Spirit, making the finished work of Christ a present reality in our lives, all attempts at spiritual discipline will be to no avail. On the other hand, deliverance is temporary at best unless it is lived out day by day. Galatians 5:16 states: ". . . live by the Spirit, and you will not gratify the desires of the sinful nature."

Lust is overcome as we consistently practice self-denial through faith in the finished work of Christ. In actual practice this is more practical than spiritual. By that I mean, it is nothing so ethereal as simply "praying through," or claiming the promises of God, or anything like that. It simply means exercising our will to refuse sin's alluring enticements, with the certain knowledge that in Christ we are free to do that — we have the power to overcome!

However, we must act quickly. Temptation must be dealt with the moment it rears its ugly head. To delay is to succumb. And if we ever allow it to take root, we have lost that battle. Not the war necessarily, but definitely the battle.

Let's return for a moment to the lay leader who came to my office to confess his bondage to pornography and prostitution. In order to remain free there were certain things he couldn't continue to do, certain places he couldn't go, not because they were sinful in themselves, but because of his propensity for sin. For instance, he could not go to a convenience store; the risk was simply too great. Nor could he go to a place that rented videos. Extreme? Perhaps, but we were dealing with matters of life and death. Jesus said: "If your right eye causes you to sin, gouge it out and throw it away. It is better for you to lose one part of your body than for your whole body to be thrown into hell" (Matt. 5:29).

Along this same line, Randy Alcorn, who is pastor of small-group ministries at Good Shepherd Community Church, Gresham, Oregon, relates something another overcomer found effective. This particular man travels extensively, so whenever he checks into a hotel, where he plans to stay for three or four days, he asks the hotel staff to please remove the television set from his room. Invariably they look at him like he's crazy and then they say, "But sir, if you don't want to watch it, you don't have to turn it on." Since he is a paying customer he politely insists that the television be removed, and he has never been refused.

He continues: "The point is, I know that in my weak and lonely moments late in the evening, I'll be tempted to watch the immoral movies that are only one push of a button away. In the past I've succumbed to that temptation over and over, but not anymore. Having the television removed in my stronger moments has been my way of saying, 'I'm serious about this, Lord,' and it's been the key to victory in my battle against impurity."[7]

Another important step is to confess your temptations and your sin to someone you can trust. The anonymous author of "The War Within: An Anatomy of Lust," first confessed his sin to a fellow minister and eventually to his wife. He writes:

"Repentance, says C. S. Lewis, 'is not something God demands of you before He will take you back and which He could let you off if He chose; it is simply a description of what going back is like.' Going back for me had to include a very long talk with my wife, who had suffered in silence and often in nescience for a decade. It was she I had wronged and sinned against, as well as God . . . . I told her nearly everything, knowing I was laying on her a burden she might not be able to carry . . . . Far smaller things had fractured our marriage for months. Somehow, she incarnated the grace of God for me . . . . She took on my enemy as her enemy too. She took on my thirst for purity as her thirst too. She loved me, and as I type this even now, tears streak my face because that love, that awesome love is so incomprehensible to me, and so undeserved."[8]

Over the years it has been my experience that temptation, which flourishes in secret, somehow loses much of its mesmerizing power when it is confessed and exposed to the light of Christian love. As spiritual leaders, then, we must take the responsibility for modeling transparency in order to create a climate where sin can be confessed and forgiven. As we acknowledge our struggles and temptations, others will feel free to confess their needs without fear of rejection or misunderstanding. On the other hand, by pretending to always "have it all together," we contribute to the conspiracy of silence which leaves us isolated and alone, terribly vulnerable to the attack of thc enemy.

If we, as individual churchmen, and if the Church as a whole, is serious about rectifying these transgressions, as well as preventing future ones, then we must be about the business of establishing a spiritual network, a support system, through which we can encourage and strengthen one another.

Additionally, it is imperative that the Church take official action to provide a confidential forum where ministers can confess their temptations, even their sinful failures, without fear of recrimination. Should such confession not result in rehabilitation, or should the minister's indiscretion become public knowledge, then appropriate disciplinary action could be taken. Unfortunately, as things now stand, a minister cannot seek help without risking public exposure and temporary suspension (usually one to two years). As a consequence, many ministers struggle alone, in fear and secrecy, until they finally overcome — or until their sins come to light. While most of us recognize the difference between a brother who voluntarily confesses and one who continues in his sin until he is caught, there seems to be little difference in the way they are now disciplined. This must be changed.

By failing to provide a working model for confidential rehabilitation, the Church has unintentionally contributed to the conditions which have resulted in moral failures like the Jimmy Swaggart tragedy. Ultimately the minister must take full responsibility for his actions; still, if our purpose is to effect redemptive change rather than simply affix blame, then we must look beyond the individual sin to the circumstances which contributed to them. And we must address these issues quickly lest others too become casualties in this lonely war with lust.

Footnotes

[1]Name Withheld, "The War Within: An Anatomy of Lust," *Leadership* (Fall Quarter, 1982), p. 31.

[2]Richard Exley, *Blue-Collar Christianity* (Tulsa: Honor Books: A Division of Harrison House, 1988).

[3]*Christianity Today*, March 18, 1988, p. 48.

[4]Jimmy Swaggart, "The Lord Of Breaking Through," *The Evangelist* (Mar. 1988, Vol. 20, No. 3), p. 7.

[5]"The War Within: An Anatomy Of Lust," pp. 41,42.

[6]G. Earl Guinn, "The Resurrection of Jesus," *The Twentieth-Century Pulpit,* edited by James W. Cox (Nashville: Abingdon, 1978), p. 78.

[7]Randy Alcorn, "Strategies To Keep From Falling," *Leadership* (Winter Quarter, 1988), p. 47.

[8]"The War Within: An Anatomy of Lust," p. 45.

Chapter 2

WHEN GOOD

GOES AWRY

Let me be perfectly candid with you. Not all sexual sin is rooted in lust, at least not initially, and it is not only "bad" people who commit adultery. I once thought that was so, but more than twenty years in the pastoral ministry has convinced me otherwise.

A true pastor is, first and foremost, a people person. He may also be an administrator, directing the activities of the church. Preaching too, may be an important part of his call. But, in his heart of hearts, he is a shepherd. He understands people, enjoys being with them, takes great delight in their companionship. His greatest fulfillment comes in ministering to them, especially in a time of crisis. As a consequence, he has almost unlimited opportunity to bond with people, and that's as it should be, as long as it is carefully guarded, and done within appropriate boundaries.

To complete the picture, add the pressures of life, the disappointments, both personal and professional, plus the multiple demands of the ministry. Under the very best of circumstances it is a demanding call, expectations are usually unrealistically high, and the hours long and emotionally draining. The minister's week is jammed with staff meetings, board meetings, administrative details, civic demands, hospital calls, counseling, petty problems, weddings, funerals, and a continuing series of emergencies. Somewhere, somehow, in the midst of all of this, he must find time to prepare himself and his message for Sunday. Add to these demands the inevitable murmurings, the criticism and petty complaints, and you have a burden almost too great to bear.

It can become a "Catch-22." If things aren't going well, he may well work all the harder in a desperate effort to turn things around. On the other hand, if the church is growing, even his success may be double-edged. Any benefit is often outweighed by increased responsibilities. Either way, he has an unusual work load, a wide range of hats that he must wear, and a host of ever-changing expectations. Not to mention the often unrealistic goals he sets for himself.

What does all of this have to do with adultery? More than you might think. In fact, much pastoral indiscretion is rooted right here. Church activities frequently require the pastor to attend meetings, of one sort or another, five and six nights a week. As a consequence his marriage suffers, both by his absence, and from exhaustion when he is present. His wife may well feel abandoned, even betrayed. Dr. Dennis Guernsey, author and professor of psychology at Fuller Theological Seminary, says: "A pastor's wife is put in a terrible bind when the church becomes The Other Woman — but her husband isn't unrighteous for sleeping

34

with her. No one considers this obsession immoral; he's 'doing God's work.' "[1]

Yet for the pastor's wife, it can become an open sore, a continuing source of frustration, even resentment. Never have I heard the pain and hopelessness more graphically, more eloquently, expounded than by Walter Wangerin, Jr., author and pastor. He writes:

"What did I learn that Sunday evening in our kitchen when Thanne broke silence and burned me with my guilt? What did I hear from the small woman grown huge in her fury, half in, half out of her coat, while the daylight died outside? I learned her grievances. I heard what her life had been like for several years, though I had not known it. I saw myself through her eyes, and the vision accused me.

" '. . . You decide my whole life for me,' (she said) 'but you hardly pay mind to the decisions. You do it with your left hand, carelessly. You run me with your left hand. Everyone else gets the right hand of kindness. Everyone else can talk to you. Not me. The left hand.

" '. . . A good pastor!' she spat the words 'You are a good pastor, Wally. God knows, I wanted you to be a good pastor. But sometimes I wish you were a bad pastor, a lazy pastor, a careless pastor. Then I'd have a right to complain. Or maybe I'd have you here sometimes. A good pastor! Wally, how can I argue with God and take you from him? Wally, Wally, your ministry runs me, but you leave me alone exactly when I need you. Where are you all the time?'

"Then this is what she told me in the darkening kitchen that terrible Sunday evening. This is what she made me see: that this good pastor carried to the people of his congregation a face full of pity —

35

"— but at our dinner table my face was drained and grey. At the dinner table I heaped a hundred rules upon our children, growling at them for the least infraction. Our dinners were tense and short.

"This is what she made me see: that I could praise, could genuinely applaud, the lisping song of a child at church —

"— but I gave the merest glance to Mary's Father's Day card, in which there was a poem the girl had labored on for two weeks straight.

". . . Thanne said she knew how much I hated to visit the jail. But I went. And it never mattered what time of day or night. Yet I did nothing that I hated, nothing, at home.

"For counseling and for sermons, my words, she said, were beautiful: a poet of the pulpit. But for our bedroom conversations, my words were bitten, complaining, and unconsidered. We talked of my duties. We talked of my pastoral disappointments. Or we hardly talked at all.

". . . I was ministering. I was a whole human, active in an honorable job, receiving the love of a grateful congregation, charging out the door in the mornings, collapsing in bed at night. I was healthy in society; she was dying in a little house — and accusing herself for the evil of wanting more time from me, stealing the time from God. I laughed happily at potlucks. She cried in secret. And sometimes she would simply hold one of the children, would hold and hold him, pleading some little love from him until he grew frightened by her intensity, unable in his babyhood to redeem her terrible sins. And sometimes she cursed herself for burdening a child, and then she wondered where God had gone.

"In those days the smile died in her face. The high laughter turned dusty in her throat. Privately the woman withered — and I did not see it."[2]

Wangerin has written autobiographically, has described an experience in his own marriage; yet if the truth were known, he could have been describing any one of a hundred, a thousand, clergy couples. What wife hasn't been tempted to resent the Church, to be jealous of the time and energy it takes from her and the children? What minister hasn't felt like a divided man, torn between the expectations of his congregation and the needs of his family? She's tempted to hate the ministry, and then she feels guilty for feeling that way. He's tempted to resent her, to feel that she doesn't appreciate him or his ministry.

Without some major adjustments such a marriage is in serious trouble. She will probably withdraw, suffer in silence, or else she will throw herself into the business of being a super-mom and the perfect minister's wife. He will undoubtedly redouble his efforts, as well, in a misguided attempt to compensate for the emptiness within himself and his marriage. It's no use. Their frantic quest is ill-considered and it only leads to further disillusionment. Their problem is not the ministry but their marriage, the way they relate to each other and the unique demands placed upon their lives. And for all their efforts there's little or no improvement, they're still terribly unfulfilled, and therefore, especially vulnerable to the subtle snare of the enemy.

Temptation for him frequently comes disguised as a fulfilling relationship. David Seamands, professor of pastoral ministry at Asbury Theological Seminary says:

"We pastors really don't have a way to know whether we are successes or failures. We're trying to please a lot of people, and sometimes we don't please any. And along comes this warm, spiritual woman who affirms, affirms, affirms.

"This is what is so often confessed to me: 'But she understood me. She was the only one who affirmed me.' And that affirmation can so easily lead to closeness, then affection, then sexuality."[3]

Let me set the stage for you. The pastor is still on the young side, probably in his mid-thirties, no longer idealistic but still hopeful. The ministry hasn't really lived up to his expectations, at least his ministry hasn't. He still believes in himself, but more and more he is forced to deal with increasing self-doubt. It seems he is never free from criticism, at least not for long. Try as he might he can't please everyone. Criticism goes with the territory, he knows that, but it still eats at him. Things aren't so good at home either. Nothing to really be concerned about, but still he wishes he and his wife were closer. He wishes she was more understanding, more sensitive to his needs. A little appreciation wouldn't hurt either.

As part of his pastoral duties he begins counseling with a member of the congregation, a rather plain woman, but as the weeks go by he finds himself more and more attracted to her. "For most of us in local-church ministry," writes Pastor Bud Palmberg, "sexual temptation doesn't come painted in the lurid tones of a vamp. It comes in the quiet, gentle relationships a pastor has with people he truly loves."[4] The attraction is not based on anything so obvious as physical beauty or sexuality. It's more subtle than that. She appreciates and affirms the qualities his wife now takes for granted.

Louis McBurney, M.D., a psychiatrist and counselor who operates Marble Retreat in the Colorado Rockies for clergy and their spouses in crises, writes: "It is important for pastors and wives to realize that the dynamics of church relationships are very different from the husband/wife relationship. It is extremely easy for a woman in the church to see him as a hero. When that happens, the pastor can begin to operate according to Willie Sutton's Law ('I rob banks cause that's where the money is'). He spends time where he gets acclaim, praise, and good strokes."[5]

Occasionally she is a woman with a predetermined plan, intent on compromising the man of God, but usually she is simply a sincere person seeking help. When she comes to him, it is for counseling, nothing more. He seems like a haven in a hostile world, a safe place. At first she is guarded, careful not to share too much. But as he proves to be a perceptive and compassionate listener, she shares with increasing candor until she feels there isn't anything she can't reveal to him. Nothing physical has happened between them, no touching or hugging, but they are well on their way to having an affair. If confronted they would probably deny that, but case history after case history will bear me out. Emotional bonding is often the first step toward infidelity, and nothing facilitates such bonding faster than an emotionally deprived woman and a compassionate pastor whose marriage and personal life are unfulfilling.

According to H. Norman Wright, founder and director of Christian Marriage Enrichment, and author of more than forty books: "The need for emotional intimacy is one of the greatest reasons for the affair. Wives have said, 'What does he see in her? She's heavier than I am. I could understand a young, sexy doll, but her!' His response is, 'She listens, cares and doesn't nag! That's more important than looks or sex.' "[6]

Peter Kreitler writes in *Affair Prevention:* "Affairs begin not just for sexual reasons but to satisfy the basic need we all have for closeness, goodness, kindness, togetherness — what I call the 'ness' needs. When these needs are not met on a regular basis in a marriage, the motivation may be to find a person who will be good to us, touch us, hold us, give us a feeling of closeness. Sexual fulfillment may indeed become an important part of an extramarital relationship, but the 'ness' needs are, for most men and women I know, initially more important."[7]

This whole discussion raises, for the sincere pastor, a host of questions, none more important than: "How can I prevent this from happening to me?"

Prevention begins with our marriage. We must keep it in good repair at all costs. We must spend time together with our mate, often and regularly; share deeply, fight fair, forgive freely and truly. Now, that seems simple enough but it's not easy by any means. To love like that demands a lifelong commitment renewed day by day. We must constantly choose to give our marriage priority time and energy. Unpremeditated affairs are usually birthed in an unfulfilling marriage; consequently, if we can make our marriage all God intends it to be, we can minimize the risks of infidelity.

On a more specific note let me share some guidelines that have served Brenda and me well these past twenty-two years. We call them the "Ten Commandments for a Healthy Marriage."

1. Protect your day off at all costs and spend it together, as a couple, and as a family.

If an emergency makes it impossible for us to have our regularly scheduled time together, we reschedule another day immediately. Nothing is more important than the time we share!

2. Eat dinner together.

Even when we have a simple meal, Brenda makes it an occasion by lighting candles and turning off the T.V. Dinner conversation is a time for sharing and making memories. Issues can be dealt with at another time.

3. Go to bed together.

Nothing undermines intimacy faster than separate bedtimes. This too is a time for sharing and for touching. It's an opportunity to touch base with each other, to make sure we haven't let our hectic schedules cause us to drift apart. Without these "set" times for togetherness we might lose contact with each other in the "busyness" of life.

4. Don't hold a grudge.

If you insist on nursing yesterday's hurts, you will become a prematurely old and bitter person, forfeiting any chance you may have of enjoying the present. We've all been hurt by those we love most. Some of us more than others, I'll grant you that, but the only hope for our marriage lies in our ability to forgive and forget. Don't let past hurts rob you of today's joy!

5. Don't take separate vacations.

Shared experiences bond us together while unshared experiences distance us from one another. Time is one of the most valuable commodities in marriage, so don't spend it foolishly.

6. Never let anything rob your marriage of the sexual joy God intended.

Sex is a gift from God to be enjoyed within the holy bonds of marriage. It is designed as a means of expressing love and giving pleasure, as well as for procreation. While true intimacy is certainly more than sex, it is never less than that.

7. Pray together.

Nothing is more intimate than a person's relationship with God. When you invite your spouse to share that experience with you, you are opening the deepest part of your being to him or her. It is often threatening at first, but the rewards more than justify the effort.

8. Play together.

K.C. Cole, reporting in *Psychology Today,* writes: "All happy couples aren't alike, so there is no single litmus test for a good marriage. But if one studies couples systematically over time, it becomes apparent that many of them share a characteristic that signals, more often than not, a healthy union.

"It's nothing so obvious as a satisfying sexual relationship, or shared interests, or the habit of talking out disputes freely. It is, rather, a capacity for playfulness of a kind that transcends fun and reflects considerably more than the partners' ability to amuse each other. Private nicknames, shared jokes and fantasies, mock insults, make-believe fighting — all these might seem like mere silliness. In fact, they may stand in for, or lubricate, more complex transactions, essential but potentially painful or even destructive."[8]

9. Little things mean a lot.

In fact, they can make the difference between a mediocre marriage and a really good one. It's usually not the expensive gifts or the foreign vacations that determine the quality of a marital relationship, but the little things. A love note in his lunch box or an "unbirthday" card for her. A kind word, help with the children, a listening ear, the feeling that he/she really cares.

10. Pledge yourselves, not only to physical faithfulness, but to emotional fidelity as well.

Brenda and I are determined that our emotional needs will be fulfilled only in our marriage. We do not allow friends, family, or career to supply these "belonging needs." This we provide for each other, and it is the strength of our relationship!

Maintaining a healthy marriage does not eliminate temptation, but it does minimize its impact. When my deepest spiritual and emotional needs are met in relationship with God and my wife, I can respond as a whole person to those who seek my counsel and support. Since my needs are being fulfilled in appropriate ways, I will not need to use ministry situations as a means for establishing my value as a person. I may still be tempted, but now I can respond out of wholeness rather than need.

Another effective way of dealing with temptation is to recognize our propensity for failure and establish guidelines to protect ourselves. As inconceivable as it may seem, I am convinced that every minister is capable of adultery, given the right circumstances. When we deny our sexuality, we set ourselves up for failure. We take unnecessary risks, naively believing that it could never happen to us. The scriptures put it bluntly, ". . . if you think you are standing firm, be careful that you don't fall!" (1 Cor. 10:12).

As we noted earlier, the dynamics of counseling often prove terribly tempting, especially if the man of God is unfulfilled in his own life. Dr. Carlfred Broderick, successful marriage counselor and author, says: "I am convinced that more people get themselves into the pain of infidelity through empathy, concern and compassion than through any base motive. The world is full of lonely and vulnerable people, hungry for a sympathetic ear and a shoulder to cry on."[9] The pastor who finds himself doing a lot of counseling is especially susceptible to this kind of temptation, both by circumstance and temperament.

I know, because for a number of years I was heavily involved in pastoral counseling. In order to protect both the counselee and myself, I developed a number of guidelines. For instance, I established a set number of times that I would see a person, usually no more than six. If the situation required more than six sessions, I referred him or her to a Christian counselor, a person who specialized in the field. Not only did this protect me from forming an unhealthy emotional attachment, it also assured the counselee of the ministry his or her situation required. As pastors, we must always guard against providing services for which we are not qualified.

When I do counsel, the sessions are always very pastoral, very professional, never chummy. I only see counselees in my office and only when my secretary or another staff member is present in the office area. I will not counsel a member of the opposite sex regarding sexual matters unless her spouse is present. Nor do I telephone counselees between sessions to "see how they are doing."

I've discovered that a telephone can be a means of instant intimacy and therefore must be used with discretion.

One final caution: I only pray for counselees on the day I am going to see them. This serves a twofold purpose:

1. It protects me from burnout.

By praying for counselees only on the day I am scheduled to see them, I am able to compartmentalize their needs, thereby freeing me from the combined weight of several clients.

2. It protects me from an unhealthy emotional bonding.

Being compassionate and caring people, it is easy for us to "feel responsible" for other people's spiritual and emotional well-being, to overinvest in their lives, creating an unhealthy dependency. This feeling is continually reinforced when we pray for them daily. And as incongruent as it may seem, prayer itself can also become an incubator in which lust is born. If you find yourself attracted to a member of the opposite sex, stop praying for that person. Such prayer only fills your heart and mind with fodder for temptation.

Finally, there is the matter of confession and accountability. I remember a counseling session some years ago where I sensed a strong undercurrent of temptation. As soon as the session was over, I went to my associate pastor and confessed my feelings. When I did, I was liberated from their seductive power. As long as I kept my feelings a secret they were strangely alluring, but in the light of open confession I saw them for what they really were. Additionally, I asked my associate to hold me accountable, to make sure I did not allow myself to become emotionally involved with this woman.

I am convinced that sexual temptation is so powerful that unless we deal with it immediately it may well overwhelm us. Kings have renounced their thrones, saints their God, and spouses their lifetime partners. People have been known to sell their souls, jobs, reputations, children, marriage — they have literally "chucked everything"! When you experience temptation, expose it immediately. Tell your wife, a Christian brother, a fellow minister — get it out into the light. Expose it!

And it's important to act before you get embroiled in passion's tangled web. A forty-one-year-old pastor who found himself having an affair wrote:

"I was in a situation I never felt I'd be in. I'd always been able to handle any temptation up to that point.

"Some people say we are intellectual beings with emotions, but I'm not so sure anymore. I'm afraid we're emotional beings with intellect instead. I keep thinking about the car analogy. Intellect is the steering wheel. It's a marvelous tool as long as all four wheels are on the road and going straight. But once you go into a skid, the steering wheel is virtually useless. When the forces of emotion take over, turning the wheel doesn't change very much."[10]

David Seamands, reflecting on that, says: "Some readers may think his comments about the human emotion and the will are self-justifying, but I find them basically accurate. The intense emotional push of an affair can hardly be described. It is a compulsion. *After a certain point, the will doesn't have a chance.*"[11] (emphasis mine)

It is crucial, then, to act before the power of passion distorts reality and renders us incapable of making spiritually sound decisions. We must establish simple guidelines regarding appropriate boundaries for both ministry and relationships. For instance, experience has taught me that I should not form a close friendship with a member of the opposite sex; it's simply too dangerous. Rigid? Perhaps, but hardly when one considers the tragedies befalling so many ministers.

Even as a couple, building a relationship with another couple, we must make a conscious effort to maintain appropriate boundaries. Not infrequently a special friendship ends in adultery. Where does a relationship get off track? That's hard to pinpoint. "A situation like that develops very subtly. The process is usually so complex and deceptive that it is frequently impossible, even in retrospect, to pinpoint a single event or point in time when 'it happened.' "[12]

Two boundaries which must be carefully guarded are in the areas of personal conversation and physical contact. Dr. Richard Dobbins, founder and director of Emerge Ministries, writes: "As friendships among couples grow more intimate, there is a tendency to become too personal and permissive in discussing the sexual side of life . . . . When personal boundaries are ignored over a long period of time, the frequency and intimacy of contacts allowed between close friends can threaten to lead the best intentioned of person to an emotional 'point of no return' which can be disastrous."[13] When couples repeatedly ignore these boundaries, adultery is often the tragic consequence.

For others the journey into the spiritual and emotional pitfalls of adultery begins with some "innocent flirting" which is carefully couched in double meanings. If the one being flirted with fails to respond, or becomes offended, the person doing the flirting can protest his innocence, claiming he was misunderstood. On the other hand, if the other person responds in kind, the game is on and excitement is high. The "players" probably haven't yet made a conscious decision to commit adultery, but subconsciously they are committed to it.

Once this deadly descent begins, it rapidly progresses from one stage to the next. The potential adulterers spend significant amounts of time fantasizing about each other.*

As the "affair" progresses, these fantasies will become more and more explicit. For the minister they will often be sexual in nature, though not always; while for the woman they will usually be romantic. Ministers who find themselves involved in such a relationship often make a concentrated effort to abstain from all but the most casual physical contact in an effort to assuage their nagging sense of sin. Such efforts are largely ineffective. God is not so easily fooled. He knows the thoughts and intents of the heart.

In the next stage the potential adulterers will begin finding excuses for calling each other. They will spend extended periods of time in deep conversations — often about spiritual things or personal problems. They will create legitimate reasons for spending time together — a special church project or choir program — anything which allows them to be together.

By this time they are actively committing adultery, not physically but emotionally; that is, they are getting their "ness" needs met by someone other than their spouse.

---

*"When asked (through the confidential survey conducted by *Christianity Today*) how often they find themselves fantasizing about sex with someone other than their spouses, 6 percent (of the ministers) said daily, 20 percent said weekly, another 35 percent said monthly or a few times a year . . . ."[14]

Someone other than their spouse is satisfying their need for closeness, tenderness, and togetherness.

Next they begin to justify their relationship. First they carefully catalog every failure in their marriage. They recite their spouses' shortcomings in deadly detail. They remember and magnify every problem. Their spouse is insensitive and unresponsive. Surely God doesn't expect them to live their entire lives in such an unhappy state. With a little help from such rationalization their compatibility leads smoothly into tenderness, the tenderness to a need for privacy, the privacy to physical consolation, and the consolation straight to bed.

Once the actual act of adultery has been committed, they find themselves in a maelstrom of emotions. Guilt and fear haunt them. Their self-esteem falters. They live with the constant fear of being found out. Prayer seems impossible. How can they face God? Yet even as they writhe in remorse they are driven with excitement and desire. They hate what they are doing, but they feel powerless to stop. They vow to break it off, to go back to just being friends, but to no avail. Their good intentions are just that — good intentions — nothing more. Like moths drawn irresistibly to a flame, they seem destined to self-destruct.

As their affair progresses, the excitement wears off, while the guilt and fear increase. By now they probably feel trapped. There is no way out of the relationship without hurting the other person, yet they can't continue like this indefinitely either. Divorce is an option, but that would destroy both his ministry and his family, as well as her family. No matter what they do, someone is going to get hurt and hurt bad!

The consequences are inevitable:

"Can a man scoop fire into his lap
    without his clothes being burned?

Can a man walk on hot coals
    without his feet being scorched?

So is he who sleeps with another
    man's wife;

no one who touches her will go
    unpunished.

". . . a man who commits adultery lacks
    judgment;
whoever does so destroys himself.

Blows and disgrace are his lot,
    and his shame will never be wiped
       away."

                    Proverbs 6:27-29,32,33

Yet there is another way. Moral failure is not inevitable. Temptation can be resisted, overcome. "No temptation has seized you except what is common to man. And God is faithful; he will not let you be tempted beyond what you can bear. But when you are tempted, he will also provide a way out so that you can stand up under it" (1 Cor. 10:13).

The key to victory in the on-going war with sexual temptation is early recognition and appropriate action. Don't pretend that temptation doesn't exist — it does, for even the best among us. Most sexual temptation can be eliminated by practicing the preventative measures mentioned in this chapter: maintain an intimate relationship with God and your spouse, set appropriate boundaries, remain accountable, and expose temptation as soon as you sense its presence. Having done all of that, if temptation still persists, do what Joseph did — run for your life. (Gen. 39:12.)

Footnotes

[1]Dean Merrill, *Clergy Couples in Crisis* (Waco: Word Books Publishers, 1985), p. 55.

[2]Walter Wangerin, Jr., *As For Me And My House* (Nashville: Thomas Nelson, Inc., 1987), pp. 85-87.

[3]"Private Sins Of Public Ministry," *Leadership* (Winter Quarter, 1988), p 20.

[4]Ibid., p. 16.

[5]Merrill, p. 124.

[6]H. Norman Wright, *Seasons of a Marriage* (Ventura. Regal Books, 1982), p. 111.

[7]Peter Kreitler with Bill Bruns, *Affair Prevention* (New York: Macmillan Publishing Co, 1981), p. 68.

[8]K.C. Cole, "Playing Together: From Couples That Play," *Psychology Today* (Feb. 1982).

[9]Carlfred Broderick, *Couples* (New York: Simon and Schuster, Inc., 1979), p. 163.

[10]Merrill, p. 202.

[11]Ibid., p. 212.

[12]Richard Dobbins, "Saints in Crisis," *Grow* (Akron: Emerge Ministries, Inc., Vol. 13, Issue 1, 1984) p. 6.

[13]Ibid., pp. 4,6.

[14]"How Common is Pastoral Indiscretion?" *Leadership* (Winter Quarter, 1988), p. 13.

Chapter 3

MID-LIFE AFFAIRS

"Oscar Wilde once wrote, 'In this world, there are only two tragedies. One is not getting what one wants, and the other is getting it.' "[1] Nowhere is the truth of this axiom more apparent than in mid-life. Numerous men have achieved more success than they ever imagined possible only to discover at mid-life, at the height of their career, that they are desperately unfulfilled. This phenomenon is not uncommon in the ministry and often results in a mid-life affair.

David Seamands, professor of pastoral ministry at Asbury Theological Seminary, explains:

"Six college mates in my denomination fell morally at the height of their success. They climbed the Methodist ladder. Two were evangelists, and four were pastors. And the four pastors — in widely separate geographical locations — all had more or less gotten either the top church in the conference or very close to it. They had reached it. That was the moment when down they went. Both evangelists and three of the four pastors are now out of the ministry.

"In college, we had noticed these guys had what we called, for want of a better term, 'unsurrendered egos.' They were gifted people. We could tell they were going to be ladder climbers. They had goals. They lived for them. That kept them clean.

"But once you reach your goals, where do you go? What do you do when you've reached the top? They apparently concluded there was nothing else to do, and they went wrong sexually. I've often wondered, however, why all six of these strong and successful ministers fell.

"A phrase from C.S. Lewis keeps running through my mind — 'the sweet poison of a false infinite.' It's a beautiful phrase. They had a false goal: *If I achieve that, I've made it.* That's a false infinite. It's sweet, and it gave them the strength to climb the ladder, but when they got to the top, they didn't have the strength to stay there. They fell off. Maybe they self-destructed. But they all did it morally. They got involved with women significantly involved in the church ministry."[2]

What is described here is not unique to the Methodist Church. I've observed the same thing in my own movement, and I'm sure the same thing is occurring in other denominations as well. Highly successful ministers are falling prey to immorality at an alarming rate. Nor is it simply a coincidence that they have succumbed to the tender trap during mid-life, at the height of their careers. By now they have probably achieved more "success" than they ever dreamed possible, and with it more frustration. The minister may be thinking that this isn't how he's supposed to feel. Where's the fulfillment, the satisfaction? Who is there to share his achievements? He is probably not intimate with his wife, not even close, and his children are strangers, grown and gone, making a life of their own.

If his public ministry is any indication of his work habits, then it's safe to conclude that he is a confirmed workaholic who thinks nothing of putting in eighty to ninety hours a week. Suddenly, at mid-life, he realizes the futility of it all, but he's at a loss to make a change. He doesn't know anything else. Lonely and depressed, he's especially vulnerable to the temptations of a mid-life affair.

Daniel Levinson, author of *The Seasons of A Man's Life,* is careful to differentiate between this type of extramarital relationship and what he calls "the kind of casual affairs" men have just for "kicks" when they are younger. He says, "People (who are in the midst of a mid-life crisis) enter an affair because *they feel that something important is missing* in their marriage and they are looking to find it elsewhere."[3] (emphasis mine) In the case of the minister it is not just his marriage that is found lacking, but his entire life and ministry. While this crisis occurs during mid-life it is really the result of choices he has been making his entire life.

It has been pointed out that human lives are generally made up of three components. First, there is the vocational: a person's career. Second, there is the relational: one's interaction with "significant others" — spouse, children, parents, and peers. Third, there's the realm of inwardness: the part of one's self that is genuinely unique and is expressed simply for his or her own private delight. I would like to add a fourth component: the spiritual — one's relationship with God. It has been suggested that all of us tend to overinvest in one or the other of these components in our earlier years and that during the mid-adult crisis, the effects of this imbalance begin to surface.

While the term "mid-life crisis" is relatively new, the experience itself is as old as mankind. There are several cases in the scriptures, but none is as obvious as the case involving King David.[4] In modern terms he would probably be called a workaholic. In five short decades he rose from the obscurity of tending sheep to become the uncontested ruler of a huge area stretching from the Nile to the Euphrates. Many factors contributed to his success, including the anointing of God; but let's not overlook his remarkable ability to give himself completely to the task at hand. He did not do it for selfish reasons either; but the cost at mid-life was extravagant just the same.

David shows us how to make a difference in the world by investing ourselves totally in our careers, our ministry. Unfortunately there was not concomitant growth on the other frontiers of his life. When we examine his biography it becomes evident that his overinvestment in the vocational area led to tragic neglect in the other facets of his existence.

Sounds frighteningly familiar, doesn't it?

After Jonathan's death there is no indication that David ever established a relationship of authentic intimacy with any other person. He had many wives but no deep relationship, and as a result he grew lonelier and lonelier as the years went by. His failure in the area of intimacy extended to his children as well. He had a number of them: the Bible lists at least nineteen sons, and there is no telling how many daughters there were. From the way they later fought and connived and betrayed each other, it seems clear that they had little contact with, or guidance from, their famous father.

Initially it is much easier, as David undoubtedly found out, to substitute the creation of several superficial relationships for the task of building one master relationship in life, but the outcome is not the same. Apparently every time he had difficulty with one of his wives, instead of using the occasion to deepen and strengthen their bond, David slid off sideways and began a new marriage. Ultimately this behavioral pattern resulted in moral failure of the gravest kind.

One spring David decided to remain in Jerusalem rather than going to battle with his armies. Perhaps he was in the midst of his mid-life crisis, painfully evaluating his life in terms of meaningfulness and fulfillment. Maybe this once he stayed at home because he wanted to begin to develop the relational area of his life. That being the case, he was surely disappointed. His wives and his children had all learned long ago to fare for themselves. He was a stranger to them and they had little feeling for him.

All of that simply suggests that the forces which drove David to have an affair with Bathsheba did not begin the night he caught sight of her bathing. They began years earlier when he gave himself exclusively to his career, ignoring his need for deep interpersonal relationships, as well as his need to develop his personal uniqueness and his relationship with God.

What can we learn from all of this? Much I hope, for the integrity of our ministry, and our marriage, may well depend on it.

H. Norman Wright, in his book *Seasons of a Marriage*, has identified two primary causes of the male mid-life crisis. The first is what he calls a "goal-gap mid-life crisis." "This refers to the distance a man perceives between the goals he has set for himself and the achievements he has actually attained."[5] In other words, at mid-life, a man is often brought face to face with reality. Not only have the goals he set for himself not been attained, but he realizes that in all likelihood he never will attain them. This can be a most distressing realization, especially if his ministry has been the foundation of his personal identity.

The most classic example I know, of this "goal-gap mid-life crisis," involved a forty-year-old pastor. His situation and his symptoms were classic. His fortieth birthday was traumatic and shortly thereafter he dyed his hair, lost more than thirty pounds, bought a new "mod" wardrobe, and returned to college. Those of us who knew him were more amused than concerned; after all his "crisis" was not serious. I mean, he could have left his church, bought a motorcycle, and headed for the West Coast. In retrospect, I now realize that we should have taken him more seriously. His new clothes and return to college were just the tip of the iceberg. The months that followed produced one disconcerting disclosure after another.

First was an incident involving a young woman, a member of his congregation, who accused him of kissing her when she came to him for counseling. He denied it, of course, and we all laughed it off as being totally out of character for him. There were other symptoms too, which are obvious in retrospect: a growing disillusionment with the ministry, talk about a new career in business, a sudden interest in rock music. Ultimately he left the church and his wife, after becoming involved with a woman fifteen years younger than he. It's not unusual for a man to feel frustrated and unfulfilled when he comes face to face with the harsh realization that he is never going to achieve the ministry goals he set for himself.

Most ministers, however, respond in a positive way once they have gotten over the initial shock. Many cope by establishing more realistic goals and by reordering the priorities in their lives. Spiritual character becomes more important than success in the ministry, relationships of more value than status symbols like church appointments, membership or salary. As a result, the mid-adult years are often the most fulfilling years of their lives.

The second cause that Wright identifies is on the opposite end of the spectrum. He writes: "Some men experience a career crisis because . . . they have attained their goals."[6] There are no more worlds to conquer. Suddenly the middle-aged minister finds himself king of the mountain, only to discover that the top of the mountain is an awfully lonely place. In his single-minded quest for success he has ignored his family and alienated his friends. Now he has everything he ever wanted, only he doesn't feel the way he's supposed to feel. Where's the inner contentment? Where's the sense of achievement? Belatedly he realizes that success without someone to share it with is not success at all. Achievement without relationships is empty indeed!

What happens next depends not only on the way that he responds to this crisis, but on his wife's response as well. While he has been busy with the work of the ministry, she has been investing her life in the family — doing what has been expected of her by others: the church, the children, even her husband. Now she is experiencing a mid-life crisis of her own, and, if not a crisis, at least some significant mid-life changes. The children are grown, her primary work as a mother is nearing completion, and she now turns her attention toward a career of her own. Wright says, "(In mid-life) Women tend to become more autonomous, aggressive and cognitive. They now seek more instrumental roles such as a career, money, influence."[7] Their husbands, on the other hand, have finally seen the futility of a life lived only for the ministry and they are now ready to re-establish contact with their mates. Rather than being affirmed and excited by their husband's sudden interest, many wives may see it as just another way of keeping them in "their place."

It's a sad picture indeed, and an all too familiar one. A lot of marital tragedy takes place right here. Just as the minister is turning toward his wife in search of intimacy and closeness, she turns away from him toward a new career, new interests in life. They are like ships passing in the night, and it is not hard to imagine what happens next. In the course of his pastoral duties he finds himself counseling with an estranged wife. Her inner emptiness mirrors his own, and, almost without realizing it, an emotional bond is formed. For the first time, in longer than he can remember, he feels alive. Here's a woman who appreciates him as a man, as a person. She listens to him and really cares about the things he's feeling. In a matter of weeks, sometimes just days, they find themselves involved in a torrid affair.

This mid-life affair actually started years ago and initially had almost nothing to do with sex. He overinvested in his work, his ministry, at the expense of his relationship with his family, his wife, and (as odd as it may seem) his relationship with God.

Gordon MacDonald, author of *Ordering Your Private World,* and past president of InterVarsity Christian Fellowship, is a tragic example of a minister who fell prey to a mid-life affair. I refer to him by name, not to cause him or his family further pain, but only that we may learn from his failures. In an interview with *Christianity Today*

(July 10, 1987) he urges us to ". . . take a hard look at what happened to me (MacDonald) and resolve that it won't happen to . . . (you)."[8]

In that same interview he identifies some of the circumstances which contributed to his adultery. He was in mid-life, at the height of his career, and for years he had driven himself. He says, "From about 1982 on I was desperately weary in spirit and in body. I was working harder and enjoying it less . . . . In addition, I now realize I was lacking in mutual accountability through personal relationships. We need friendships where one man regularly looks another man in the eye and asks hard questions about our moral life, our lust, our ambitions, our ego."[9]

The first step then, in avoiding a mid-life affair is to invest ourselves proportionately in the four main areas of our lives — vocational, relational, personal, and spiritual.*

As I've already noted most of us tend, during our early years, to overinvest in at least one of these areas at the expense of the others, and then we suffer the consequences at mid-life. In the case of the minister, as in the case of most men, he tends to pour himself into his work. It's easy to justify the long hours, the evenings away from the family, the intense schedule. He's doing the Lord's work. And herein lies the trap — the Lord's work is never done.

The ministry never has been and never will be a nine-to-five job, but the minister had better find a way to manage his life or he will suffer the consequences. The answer, I believe, is in living a God-centered life rather than a need-

---

* For a complete treatment of this subject please refer to *The Rhythm of Life* by Richard Exley (Honor Books: A Division of Harrison House, Tulsa, Oklahoma, 1987).

centered life. "Compassion born only out of sympathy for suffering humanity risks both the extremes of fanaticism and burnout. Healing compassion, on the other hand, combines the love and guidance of the Creator with a genuine concern for the hurting in our world. If our only motivation is need, we will be swallowed up, we will risk becoming part of the problem rather than part of the solution. Our only hope is to let God define our area of responsibility and then to live within our limits, both emotionally and physically."[10]

When a minister overinvests in his work, for an extended period of time, at least two things happen. First, he distances himself from his wife and family. The relationship that should be at the center of his being gets shoved to the ragged edge. His marriage gets the leftovers, the scraps at the end of a demanding day, hardly the stuff of which meaningful marriages are made. And when his marriage is not in good repair, it goes without saying, that he is susceptible to an affair. Following MacDonald's resignation he was asked what he had done to restore his marriage relationship. He replied, "It's not as much finding things to do as it is *taking the necessary time,* because for people in ministry, the work is never over."[11] (emphasis mine)

Which brings us to the second consequence — he wears out! MacDonald said, ". . . I was desperately weary in spirit and in body."[12] Consequently, when he struggles with temptation, he has neither the inner strength nor the relational resources to resist. He succumbs, I think, oftentimes more out of an inner emptiness than any evil desire.

Let me share an insight which has been helpful to me. The first clue to burnout, and the spiritual and emotional exhaustion which accompanies it, is a lack of inner fulfillment. By experience, I have discovered that I can remain publicly effective long past the point where my work has ceased to be inwardly fulfilling. In fact, I can continue to minister with surprising proficiency even as I begin to resent my work and the very people I am called to serve. If I ignore this warning signal, serious trouble is dead ahead. If, on the other hand, I heed this early warning and take the steps necessary to bring my life back into balance, I can soon return to the ministry with a renewed enthusiasm.

Another misconception which sets up the minister for the mid-life affair is the confusion about his identity, his self-worth. Many ministers labor a lifetime believing that if they can just reach their goals they will finally feel accepted, worthy. Not true! There is not enough success in the world to quiet the discordant voices within. Self-esteem is not the by-product of achievement, but the natural consequence of a healthy relationship with one's parents, peers and, of course, God. It is a matter of who you are in Christ, not what you have done. Tragically, the minister who labors a lifetime, only to discover he has chased a pipe dream, often becomes a prime candidate for the mid-life affair.

None of us is immune to sexual temptation, and as I look back over my life I realize that the times I struggled the hardest were those times when my relationships were most in need of repair. Not just my relationship with Brenda, but also my relationships with godly men. This too is borne out in MacDonald's experience, and he is now working to shore up this area of his life as well. He said, "We also have begun to cultivate friendships on a much deeper level than in the past. And I have deliberately cultivated the friendships of three or four godly men."[13]

If you pastor in a remote, isolated area you are probably thinking: "That's an impossibility for me. There are not three or four godly men in a hundred-mile radius. Why, the nearest pastor in my denomination is over fifty miles away."

Believe me, I know what you're talking about. For years I pastored small churches in remote areas, and it was extremely difficult to build friendships with men who shared my interests in the things of God. As a result, I was often lonely and restless. In desperation I tried to make Brenda my only friend. I inundated her with things about my ministry, my day, my dreams, and then experienced disappointment and frustration when she responded with less than the expected enthusiasm. This, of course, strained our relationship. I was placing on her a burden too great for her to bear. She was my best friend, but now I was asking her to be my only friend. In short, my need was greater than her resources, a situation which frustrated me and left her feeling inadequate.

Thankfully, we received a call to become pastors of Christian Chapel in Tulsa, Oklahoma. This proved to be a major turning point in our lives. For the very first time I was surrounded by a church full of men who were deeply committed to the things of God. They shared my love for the scriptures and the work of the kingdom, and I have been able to build a number of significant friendships. These relationships have stood me in good stead on numerous occasions. These men hold me accountable, strengthen me when I am weak, correct me when I am wrong and love me at all times. Interestingly enough, these friendships have also contributed significantly to my relationship with Brenda as well. Now that she is freed from the burden of being my *only* friend, she is free to be my *best* friend, and she is!

The key element in developing relationships that last is time. Whether we are talking about marriage or friendship, the key is the same — time! It's demanding, I'll grant you that, but the returns justify the investment many times over. God only knows how many times I've escaped the tempter's snare through the counsel and prayers of a special friend. Hopefully, I've contributed as significantly to others' lives as well. Solomon said:

"Two are better than one,
　　because they have a good return for
　　　their work:
If one falls down,
　　his friend can help him up.
But pity the man who falls
　　and has no one to help him up!
Also, if two lie down together, they
　　　will keep warm.
　But how can one keep warm alone?
Though one may be overpowered,
　　two can defend themselves.
A cord of three strands is not quickly
　　broken."

Ecclesiastes 4:9-12

If you are pastoring a small church in a remote area, don't despair. You are isolated, but you are not alone. Think of those special relationships you built while in Bible college or seminary. Those friends are as near as your telephone. Granted, that's not like seeing them face to face, but it sure beats self-pity for company. What about a favorite professor, your spiritual mentor, the pastor of the church you attended before you entered full-time ministry? In order for these relationships to be as constructive as possible, you will need to keep in touch regularly, probably at least once a week. Fit it into your budget. It's mandatory!

Look beyond your own denominational borders. One of the best friends I've ever had is a Methodist minister who reached out to Brenda and me, when we were just kids pastoring our first church, in a little place called Holly, Colorado. His friendship made two of the most difficult years of our lives not only bearable, but blessed. My life and ministry bear the imprint of his influence still, almost twenty years later. Many times since I've wished I could find another friend like him. I've even prayed to that end. Gently the Lord rebukes me, "Don't pray, 'Let me find a friend like that.' Instead pray, 'Let me be a friend like that.' "

And finally, in order to avoid a mid-life affair, we need to maintain our relationship with God. How, you may be wondering, can someone whose entire life revolves around the things of God, lose his relationship with the Lord? It's not a problem of absence as much as it is a problem of overfamiliarity. And we are constantly in danger of substituting this familiarity for intimacy. Prayer becomes a public duty, done without pleasure; rather than a private experience, a spiritual discipline, which nurtures the soul. We handle the Word of God the way a carpenter handles his tools. They're the instruments of his trade, but not necessarily sacred.

The answer does not lie in separating what we do for God from our relationship with God. That would simply make us professionals, in the worst sense of the word —

hirelings. No, true ministry is an expression of who we are in God, but we must always guard against confusing what we do for God with our relationship to Him. The ministry is not a profession, it's a calling. If it were a profession, then work would be of utmost importance; but since it's a calling, nothing is more important than our relationship with the Lord, and we must protect it at all costs.

At this time in my life I suppose my greatest temptation lies right here. The demands of ministry tempt me to overcommit myself, and when I do, I end up physically and emotionally exhausted. A recent entry in my journal is a case in point:

"Lord,
It's not daylight yet
and I'm alone in this shadowy sanctuary.
A gentle and much needed rain
makes a friendly sound on the roof.
I'm so thankful to be here,
  alone with You,
    together again.

"The last four or five weeks
have been especially hard.
I've traveled nearly 10,000 miles
and preached close to forty times.
The ministry has been great,
but now I'm empty, drained.
I need solitude, quiet,
  time alone . . .
    away from the press of people.

"Much of it is my own fault.
I haven't yet learned
to maintain the rhythm of life

while on the road.
Everything suffers . . .
   my devotional life succumbs
      to the press of public ministry
         two and three times a day.
Solitude is crowded out by fellowship,
   and fellowship itself is lost
      in polite conversation,
   drowned in the constant clamor
      of endless questions.

"By the end of the scheduled meetings
I'm just going through the motions,
at least that's the way it seems to me.
Your anointing makes the public ministry
effective,
   but on the inside I'm tired and unfulfilled.
      I'm tired of preaching and praying,
         tired of talking and smiling,
   tired of the sound of my own voice,
      tired of me!

"Which brings me back to the present,
   this dim sanctuary,
      quiet except for the sound of the rain.
This solitude . . .
You don't press me.
   You seem content to let me
      savor the silence.
To let me enjoy Your presence
   without demands.

"Thanks, Lord!
I needed this time
   to be still,
      to be renewed.

"Amen."

The time to prepare for mid-life is right now! In order to remain effective in ministry and avoid a mid-life affair, we must develop a network of spiritual friends, a support system, with our spouse at the very center. We must set realistic goals which we can attain but not outgrow. Our identity must be firmly rooted in who we are in Christ rather than what we have done. And finally we must maintain a personal relationship with the living God.

If we do this faithfully, for a lifetime, we will have nothing to fear when mid-life's inevitable storms come.

" 'Therefore everyone who hears these words of mine and puts them into practice is like a wise man who built his house on the rock. The rain came down, the streams rose, and the winds blew and beat against that house; yet it did not fall, because it had its foundation on the rock. But everyone who hears these words of mine and does not put them into practice is like a foolish man who built his house on sand. The rain came down, the streams rose, and the winds blew and beat against that house, and it fell with a great crash.' "

Matthew 7:24-27

Footnotes

[1]Harold Kushner, *When All You've Ever Wanted Isn't Enough* (New York: Summit Books: A Division of Simon & Schuster, Inc., 1986), p. 3.

[2]"Private Sins of Public Ministry," *Leadership* (Winter Quarter, 1988), p. 21.

[3]*U.S. News & World Report* (Oct. 25, 1983), p. 74.

[4]Much of the insight for this discussion of David and mid-life was inspired by *Stages: The Art of Living the Expected* by John Claypool (Waco: Word Books, Publisher, 1977).

[5]H. Norman Wright, *Seasons of a Marriage* (Ventura: Regal Books: A Division of Gospel Light Publications, 1982), p. 62.

[6]Ibid., p. 64.

[7]Ibid., p. 57.

[8]"A Talk with the MacDonalds," *Christianity Today* (July 10, 1987), p. 39.

[9]Ibid., p. 38.

[10]Richard Exley, *The Rhythm of Life* (Tulsa: Honor Books: A Division of Harrison House, 1987), p. 181.

[11]*Christianity Today* (July 10, 1987), p. 38.

[12]Ibid.

[13]Ibid., pp. 38,39.

Chapter 4

THE PERILS OF POWER

"Lord,
I'm deeply troubled
by the arrogance and carnality
I see in the ministry.
Wealth is no longer a blessing
but a right!
Your name is misused for personal gain.
The trappings of worldly success
have become the measurement of ministry.
Lust and greed,
poorly disguised,
now traffic where holy simplicity
once reigned.
Duplicity and double-talk
have replaced personal integrity.
Rationalization and self-justifying logic —
'the ends justify the means' kind of theology —
have become the 'gospel' of our day.
I want to lift my voice,

I want to cry out in protest;
yet even as I do
I sense an equally sinister spirit within.
Self-righteousness tempts me
to become judgmental and critical.
My voice,
raised in holy protest,
sounds shrill and divisive
even to my own ears.
Help me, Lord, help me!"

_____

"My child —
Your concerns are well justified,
both for the ministry,
and for yourself.
It's not easy being a prophetic voice;
and you're right,
the greatest danger,
the greatest temptation,
is to become self-righteous and judgmental.
There is no cure-all,
no safe place,
where you are immune to temptation;
but there are some principles
which will protect your heart.
First, always remember I love 'them'
as much as I love you.
They are not the enemy to be attacked,
but brothers to be restored.
You must always be careful to differentiate
between the issue and the individual.
You can hate the issue,
attack it and denounce it,

but you must love the individual.
Issues can be dealt with publicly.
Individuals must be confronted privately.
And finally,
guard your heart, your motives,
lest you become a monster
in order to destroy one."

I wrote that prayer (prayed it really) and recorded it in my journal, on July 8, 1987, almost four months after the PTL scandal first broke. I was grieving then as I am now. In truth, I believe I had seen it coming for months, for perhaps as long as two years. Nothing specific, no dates or details, just a certain sense that all was not right. I did not rejoice in that knowledge then, nor do I now. I wish I had been wrong. I wish there had been no excesses, no moral failures, no sin. Even now I want to put it behind me. I am tempted to pretend it didn't happen, to simply forgive and forget, but the Spirit will not allow it. He is requiring something more of His Church than unconditional love and forgiveness. Not less than that, but more.

This is a situation which must be dealt with, rectified. The Church must address these issues, not just the obvious sins of certain individuals, but the underlying causes as well. We must learn how to use televangelism and the power it brings, or it will destroy us one by one.

The March 18, 1988 issue of *Christianity Today* had a column entitled a "Year to Forget" which chronicled the events following the disclosure of the PTL scandal:

"March 19, 1987: Jim Bakker, confessing adultery, resigns from PTL; announces he is turning the ministry over to Jerry Falwell.

"April 28, 1987: Richard Dortch, PTL president, is dismissed by Falwell following revelations of his role in a cover-up attempt.

"May 4, 1987: Bakker and Dortch lose their credentials as Assemblies of God ministers.

"June 12, 1987: PTL declares bankruptcy.

"August 1987: A federal grand jury begins investigating PTL records to determine if Bakker and his former top aides are guilty of mail fraud and tax evasion.

"September 9, 1987: The Bakkers file a claim against PTL for a minimum of $1.3 million in money they say PTL owes them.

"October 8, 1987: Falwell and his board resign from PTL a day after a court rules that PTL creditors and partners may file their own reorganization plan.

"November 1, 1987: David Clark assumes duties as PTL's bankruptcy trustee.

"December 16, 1987: The Internal Revenue Service, in an effort to revoke PTL's tax-exempt status, claims the Bakkers and other top PTL officials received almost $15 million in excessive compensation from 1981 to 1987. A judge's restraining order temporarily prevents revocation of tax-exempt status.

"December 22, 1987: The reorganization plan submitted by PTL's new leadership is approved in bankruptcy court.

"February 1, 1988: The new PTL leadership files a $52 million counterclaim against the Bakkers and top aide David Taggart, based on overcompensation and mismanagement.

"May 2, 1988: The newly reorganized PTL is scheduled to begin operating; it is also the deadline for raising over $4 million above operating expenses."[1]

I reiterate the PTL incident and the events which followed, not to reopen old wounds or to cast further doubts, but only as a graphic example of the perils of power. And if that is not enough to convince you of the tremendous temptations inherent in the power which comes with being the head of a national T.V. ministry, consider the sexual transgressions of Jimmy Swaggart, the questionable fund-raising tactics of many television evangelists, and the charges and counter-charges they hurled at each other during the so called "holy wars." This is hardly the conduct one would expect from men of God.

Are these evil men, charlatans? Hardly. They are good men, godly men, who suddenly found themselves the stewards of tremendous power. A power comprised of vast sums of money and international visibility. Listener contributions totaling, in some cases, as much as $170 million annually; and enormous popularity — the PTL network once reached into 14 million homes daily while Jimmy Swaggart was heard weekly in 143 countries. Imagine all of that with little or no real accountability. The temptations they must have experienced are beyond the realm of comprehension for most of us.

Following the public disclosure of Jimmy Swaggart's sexual indiscretion, Rice University sociologist and longtime Swaggart commentator William Martin said: "I thought (Swaggart) was one of the most honest and sincere preachers I had ever met. But I've seen him change over the years. He really seems to have been seduced by the power and the fame."[2] Richard Dortch, second in command at PTL

75

when news of that scandal broke, concludes: "A television camera can change a preacher quicker than anything else . . . . It turns good men into potentates . . . . It's so easy to get swept away by popularity: Everybody loves you, cars are waiting for you, and you go to the head of the line. That's the devastation of the camera. It has made us less than what God has wanted us to become."[3]

The temptations that come with power are not unique to televangelists, just more pronounced. For years I pastored small churches in rural areas, yet I (who had no real power, at least by world standards) too struggled with its intoxicating deception. Like the twelve, I wanted to be the greatest in the kingdom, and I wanted all the "perks" that came with it. I justified my ambition by interpreting it as a vision for the kingdom, a divine call for my life, God's will; and herein lies part of the deception. I was committed to the kingdom, I did care about reaching the world with the Gospel, but it was all tangled up with my own ego needs.

As disconcerting as it may be, the fact is that ambition and obedience will probably always share the seat of power in the minister's life. It's not ideal, but it is, I think, a realistic appraisal of the minister and the ministry. Our salvation does not come in totally divorcing ourselves from personal ambition, that's virtually impossible, but in recognizing it for what it is and honestly dealing with it. The real trouble starts when we experience success and interpret that as divine approval for all of our motives. When that happens there's little or nothing left to restrain our ambitious egos.

When I think of the perils of power, when I think of a man ruined by success, the first person who comes to mind is Saul, Israel's first king. When we first meet Saul, on the pages of holy scripture, he is a winsome man, physically attractive, standing ". . . a head taller than any of the others" (1 Sam. 9:2), yet gifted with the grace of humility, " '. . . small in . . . (his) . . . own eyes . . .' " (1 Sam. 15:17), to use the language of the scriptures. He says, after Samuel informs him that he has been chosen king, " '. . . am I not a Benjamite, from the smallest tribe of Israel, and is not my clan the least of all the clans of the tribe of Benjamin? Why do you say such a thing to me?' " (1 Sam. 9:21). Even after Samuel has anointed him king he remains unaffected, and on the day of his coronation he cannot be found, for he is hiding ". . . among the baggage" (1 Sam. 10:22).

How different from the power-hungry despot whose jealousy drove him mad and sent him into murderous rages. What, I ask you, changed this gifted and humble man into a paranoid powermonger? The answer in a word is *power*. It has been said that power corrupts and absolute power corrupts absolutely, for history is filled with a long line of Sauls. Fine men, brilliant men, even godly men, who were corrupted by the deceitfulness of power.

Saul's degeneration took place over a period of years and was first the work of independence, then pride and disobedience. Initially he made himself accountable to Samuel, he sought his counsel and obeyed his instructions. His first rallying cry to the nation of Israel was, "...'This is what will be done to the oxen of anyone who does not follow *Saul* and *Samuel*' " (1 Sam. 11:7). (emphasis mine) As time progressed, however, Saul became more and more independent, he began to take matters into his own hands, even disobeying the direct counsel of the prophet. When Samuel confronted him, Saul tried to justify his behavior by saying that the circumstances were pressing and therefore extraordinary measures were necessary. " '...*I felt compelled*

to offer the burnt offering' " (1 Sam. 13:12), he explained
to Samuel. (emphasis mine)

" 'You acted foolishly,' Samuel replied. 'You have not
kept the commandment the LORD your God gave you; if
you had, he would have established your kingdom over
Israel for all time. But now your kingdom will not endure;
the LORD has sought out a man after his own heart and
appointed him leader of his people, because you have not
kept the LORD's command' " (1 Sam. 13:13,14).

It's interesting to note that Saul never acknowledged
his foolishness in any way. In his mind he had simply done
the expedient thing. Disobedient, yes; but expedient. A kind
of "the ends justify the means" type of thinking: "Samuel
is old, belonging to another generation; he doesn't
understand the demands of kingship. As a leader I have
to seize control, take responsibility, make decisions."

Tragically it is only a small step from foolish
independence to sinful disobedience.

Some years later the Lord directed Samuel to tell Saul
to utterly destroy the Amalekites. " 'Do not spare them;
put to death men and women, children and infants, cattle
and sheep, camels and donkeys' " (1 Sam. 15:3). And again
Saul disobeyed, only this time it was not born of foolishness,
but rebellion. To the King's way of thinking it seemed such
a waste to slaughter all of that prize livestock. And why
kill King Agag when he could be used for propaganda
purposes?

When confronted, Saul once again refuses to accept
the responsibility for his disobedience. First he blames the
soldiers, " '...they spared the best of the sheep and cattle

to sacrifice to the LORD your God, but we totally destroyed the rest' " (1 Sam. 15:15).

" 'Stop!' Samuel said to Saul.... '...Why did you not obey the LORD? Why did you *pounce on the plunder* and do evil in the eyes of the LORD?' " (1 Sam. 15:16,19). (emphasis mine)

Again Saul hedges, attempts to justify his own disobedience, attempts to cloak his sinful self-interests with "spiritual" rationalization.

" 'But I did obey the LORD,' Saul said. 'I went on the mission the LORD assigned me. I completely destroyed the Amalekites and brought back Agag their king. The soldiers took sheep and cattle from the plunder, the best of what was devoted to God, in order to sacrifice them to the LORD your God at Gilgal.'

"But Samuel replied:
" 'Does the LORD delight in burnt
    offerings and sacrifices
as much as in obeying the voice of the LORD?
To obey is better than sacrifice,
    and to heed is better than the fat of rams.
For rebellion is like the sin of divination,
    and arrogance like the evil of idolatry.
Because you have rejected the word of
        the LORD,
    he has rejected you as king.' "

1 Samuel 15:20-23

Finally, Saul acknowledges his sin; that is, he confesses it — but he does not repent.* Even now he is more worried

---

*Let it be noted that, without repentance, confession can be self-serving — nothing more than a means of invoking sympathy and understanding; a way of relieving guilt.

about his image, how he is going to look in the eyes of his people, than he is in pleasing the Lord.

"Saul replied, 'I have sinned. But please honor me before the elders of my people and before Israel; come back with me so that I may worship the LORD your God' " (1 Sam. 15:30). That is, "Don't let my sin become public knowledge. Too many people will be hurt." Tragic, isn't it, how Saul was more concerned about his public image than he was about the sin and rebellion which reigned within? His only concern, it seemed, was the possible impact his rebellion and disobedience might have on the kingdom, never realizing that the kingdom was already gone.

Then Samuel died, but his words lived on, ringing in Saul's ears, " 'The LORD has torn the kingdom of Israel from you today and has given it to one of your neighbors — to one better than you' " (1 Sam. 15:27). Those words haunted Saul, drove him mad, made him suspicious of every man, protective of his domain. His was a reign of terror fueled by fear and suspicion.

Although Saul remained in power for many more years, he was a king in name only. The anointing was gone. The Spirit of the Lord had departed from him. Nothing could save his kingdom now. " 'He who is the Glory of Israel does not lie or change his mind; for he is not a man, that he should change his mind' " (1 Sam. 15:29). Confession and repentance could have saved Saul's soul, but his kingdom was gone. Unfortunately he lived out his years in tragic defiance and died by his own hand, having lost both his soul and his kingdom.

This is more than just a Bible story, more than just a bit of ancient history; it's a word from God to the Church in this present age. Paul writes, "These things happened to them as examples and were written down as warnings for us . . ." (1 Cor. 10:11). With that thought in mind, let's re-examine Saul's tragic life in light of recent events.

First, the nation of Israel was partially responsible for Saul's tragic end. Had he never become king he may well have lived a simple life, enjoying the blessing of family and friends. We don't know that, to be sure, but we do know that there was no hint of the egomania which destroyed him until he was exposed first hand to the perils of power. Remember, Saul had no ambitions to become king. In fact, this whole business of a kingdom originated with the people themselves. They cried, ". . . 'We want a king over us. Then we will be like all the other nations, with a king to lead us and to go out before us and fight our battles' " (1 Sam. 8:19,20).

Have you ever wondered why God was so resistant to the idea of a king? What was there about it that was so "evil" in His eyes? What exactly is a king anyway? He is an absolute monarch, he answers to no one, he has power without accountability. Has there ever been a man, I wonder, or a woman, capable of handling that kind of power? I think not. Consider history — many of its bloodiest pages were written by kings and dictators, rulers who wielded power without accountability.

Now let's apply this principle to our present situation. Isn't it true that we believers, especially pentecostal and charismatic believers, take great pride in our "own" television networks, amusement parks, retirement villages, and the multi-million dollar budgets they generate and require? We point to them with pride and view them as "proof" of God's favor. The world has its celebrities and, like ancient Israel, the Church has cried until God has given us "kings" of our own. But have we considered the cost?

As I view the fallout — well-known ministers in disgrace, ministries in bankruptcy, court cases pending, charges and counter-charges — I cannot help but feel somewhat responsible. We funded it. We gave them our money without requiring financial accountability, and all the while it was destroying them.

My concern has very little to do with the actual salaries ministers are paid, or the kind of cars they drive; my concern is for them as persons, as men and women of God. How are they affected by all of the trappings of "spiritual" success? Remember, Church history is littered with the wreckage of great men brought down by spiritual pride and the misuse of power. In light of that, I believe it behooves us to do everything within our power to protect each other from these inherent dangers.

The question before us is not whether televangelism is useful or not. No one can really question that. Missionaries around the world give first-hand testimony to the effectiveness of the Jimmy Swaggart broadcasts in foreign countries, as is evidenced by his overseas crusades, which are the largest in history. Here, in the United States, thousands of people who ordinarily would not darken a church door, or ever hear a Gospel message, are being reached with the saving grace of Jesus Christ. Steve Wright says, "I pastor people whose lives have been changed by the gospel so imperfectly presented by many television evangelists."[4] Most local pastors can say the same thing. Wright then cites this example:

"They lived together in the city far from our suburban church. Unmarried. Bisexual. Promiscuous. Addicted to alcohol and drugs. He visited our church at the invitation of a friend. She refused to attend. He accepted Christ. She did not. They separated over his desire for a changed life. Two years passed — I met them again. Married. Soon to be new parents. Free from addiction and immorality. Alone she had listened soberly to a TV evangelist preaching in a perspiring rage. Every sin he named she had committed. She prayed to the Christ who receives sinners, convinced that he would accept her. Their lives will never be the same."[5]

The issue for me is how to maximize the returns for the kingdom of God while minimizing the risks for the minister. Television evangelism works, but at what cost? In the case of both Jim Bakker and Jimmy Swaggart, great good was done through their television ministries, but at a staggering cost to both them and their families — not to mention the injury which was inflicted to the Body of Christ.

A television ministry of that magnitude is not unlike a kingdom, and the evangelist wields unbelievable power. Therefore it is critically important that he surround himself with spiritually strong men who will hold him accountable, both spiritually and financially. These men must be strong enough to speak the truth in love, and wise enough to discern between the wisdom of God and their own opinion. They should also provide an inner circle of spiritual support and protection. In truth, almost all men are their own worst enemy, therefore every spiritual leader must have trusted men who will protect him from himself.

Power itself is not inherently evil, but it is dangerous. And the most dangerous power of all is that which cloaks itself in the guise of religion.

Richard Foster writes: "Power can be an extremely destructive thing in any context, but in the service of religion it is downright diabolical. Religious power can destroy in a way that no other power can . . . . Those who are a law unto themselves and at the same time take on a mantle of piety are particularly corruptible. When we are convinced that what we are doing is identical with the kingdom of God, anyone who opposes us must be wrong. When we are convinced that we always use our power to good ends, we believe we can never do wrong. But when this mentality possesses us, we are taking the power of God and using it to our own ends . . . . When pride is mixed with power the result is genuinely volatile. Pride makes us think we are right, and power gives us the ability to cram our vision of rightness down everyone else's throat. The marriage between pride and power carries us to the brink of the demonic."[6]

When Jesus came, He introduced us to a new kind of power — a selfless power married to a holy love. He voluntarily abdicated his divine rights in order to show us how to use power redemptively. In the incarnation He gave up every advantage of His divine nature and in His earthly ministry He renounced His rights as a leader in order to accept the higher calling of a servant/minister. Notice that He did not give up His responsibility as a leader — just His rights and privileges. He said of Himself, " '. . . the Son of Man did not come to be served, but to serve . . .' " (Matt. 20:28).

As has been already noted, the spiritual leader himself must take the ultimate responsibility for his destiny. He stands or falls by his own decisions. Of critical importance is his model for ministry, his perception of power and its purpose. When I entered the ministry more than twenty years ago, televangelists (as such) did not exist. Still, I saw ministers in much the same light as executives or celebrities. If the minister thinks of himself in that way, then he will expect to be served rather than look for places to serve. He will accept the amenities of success as his just due and will become resentful if they are not forthcoming.

In truth, it is but a small step from expectation to demand, and from demand to abuse.

How different from the model of the Master who took a towel and a basin of water and washed the disciples' feet. "Do nothing out of selfish ambition or vain conceit . . . ," wrote the Apostle Paul, "Your attitude should be the same as that of Christ Jesus:

"Who, being in very nature God,
    did not consider equality with God
        something to be grasped,
but made himself nothing,
    taking the very nature of a servant,
    being made in human likeness.
And being found in appearance as a
    man,
he humbled himself
and became obedient to death —
    even death on a cross!"

Philippians 2:3,5-8

Based on the example of Jesus, Who made Himself nothing, humbled Himself, and became obedient, we can only conclude that discipline and self-denial is the only way to control our lust for power. We must voluntarily limit our lifestyles in order to keep the "old man" in check. Indulge him just a little and he will demand more and more.

Richard Foster says, "Inordinate passions are like spoiled children and need to be disciplined, and not indulged."[7]

The spiritual leader who wants to keep his own ambition and lust for power in check must be willing to submit his plans and visions to the judgment of a council of godly advisers. Spiritual guidance, whether it comes in the form of an inner witness or through a personal vision, is simply too subjective to be left to his judgment alone. It is just too easy for vain ambition to cloak itself in the guise of divine direction. If his promptings are truly from the Lord then they will be confirmed by his advisers.

Another inherent danger is isolation. Experience has demonstrated that success, especially significant success, tends to isolate us from both the Body and our peers. Soon we perceive things only from our perspective, one which tends to become ingrown after a few years. In those times we need the input of an outsider, a spiritual person who sees things from a different perspective. An excellent example of this is Jethro's counsel to Moses:

". . . 'What you are doing is not good. You and these people who come to you will only wear yourselves out. The work is too heavy for you; you cannot handle it alone. Listen now to me and I will give you some advice, and may God be with you. You must be the people's representative before God and bring their disputes to him. Teach them the decrees and laws, and show them the way to live and the duties they are to perform. But select capable men from all the people — men who fear God, trustworthy men who hate dishonest gain — and appoint them as officials over thousands, hundreds, fifties and tens. Have them serve as judges for the people at all times, but have them bring every difficult case to you; the simple cases they can decide themselves. That will make your load lighter, because they will share it with you. If you do this and God so commands, you will be able to stand the strain, and all these people will go home satisfied.' "

Exodus 18:17-23

Now here's the important part: "Moses listened to his father-in-law and did everything he said" (Ex. 18:24).

Finally, the spiritual leader must live under authority. It is his responsibility to establish and maintain relationships of mutual accountability. "Nothing is more dangerous than leaders accountable to no one. We all need others who can laugh at our pomposity and prod us into new forms of obedience. Power is much too dangerous a thing for any of us to face alone. If we look at the abuses of power in the Church today, very often we will see that behind them is someone who has decided that he or she has a direct pipeline to God and therefore does not need the counsel and correction of the community."[8]

I have such a relationship with Augustine, an evangelist who ministers in the office of a prophet. About two years ago he received a vision for me while we were conducting a conference together in the Northwest.

In this vision I was on a raft with two of my board members. A large green serpent came out of the water and fastened itself onto my leg and began pulling me into the river. The board members attacked the serpent with their oars, but to little avail. Augustine himself was watching, helplessly, from the shore. Finally, he left and returned almost immediately with a lion which plunged into the river and attacked that green serpent. They fought furiously, in and out of the water, before the lion finally killed the vile reptile.

When Augustine finished sharing the vision, I asked him what it meant. He said he would rather not tell me. He thought it would be better if the Lord revealed it to me. I'm not really sure why I asked him to interpret it, I already knew what it meant. The moment he began speaking, it seemed as though a sword pierced my heart, the conviction of the Spirit was so great that I was in physical pain. That green serpent was the spirit of power, and it had fastened itself upon me. It was attempting to destroy me.

Every time I went to prayer, for the next six or seven weeks, God would reveal another area in which I had abused power. Nor were those painless revelations of insipid facts. No! Each time I literally gasped with pain. I wept in repentance before the Lord. I begged Him to change me, to create in me a new heart, a heart of humility and service. One day it was the painful memory of a terrible thing I had said to Brenda, in anger, years before. Although I had apologized, I had not realized until now how deeply I had wounded her. There in prayer, in the presence of God, it seemed her pain became mine, and with the pain, a terrible shame. Another day it was a mortal wound I had inflicted on the spirit of a young man named Terry who was part of the congregation in one of the first churches I had pastored. Then there was the day the Lord revealed the hidden depths of my critical spirit, especially toward other ministers. Day after day, week after week, it went on, this terrible soul searching, this awesome battle between the Lion of the tribe of Judah and that awful serpent called power.

I remembered a dream I had had for years. Suddenly
its meaning was frightingly clear:

"It was only a dream,
or so I had told myself.
Yet I dreamed it again and again,
at least once a month,
sometimes as often as twice a week,
for almost sixteen years.

"In my dream
Brenda was emotionally involved
with another man.
While this other man's identity
varied from dream to dream,
the theme never changed.
He was always a public figure,
rich and powerful.

"I tried to reason with her,
tried to tell her she was throwing away
a beautiful relationship
for a cheap thrill,
but I couldn't reach her.
She seemed oblivious to both
my pain and my pleas.
'It's nothing,' she insisted.
'Just something to do.'
Yet she could not be persuaded
to give up the relationship.
'I'm not doing anything,'
she explained irritably.
'We're just friends.'

"Then I would awake
feeling sick and angry.

This went on,
as I've already said,
for almost sixteen years.
I dreamed it again,
early one morning,
and when I awoke,
I went into the bathroom.
Leaning my head against the wall, I cried.
'Lord, what does this mean?'
Instantly, He answered me.
Not with an audible voice,
but with such clarity
that I could not doubt its reality.

"He said,
in a voice audible only to my spirit,
'That dream is not about Brenda.
It's about you and Me,
and you're breaking My heart.'
Although I had been actively involved
in the ministry all my adult years,
in my heart of hearts,
I had nurtured a secret fantasy.
I dreamed of being rich and powerful,
a criminal lawyer perhaps,
or a politician.
A novelist or an actor.
I had never pursued those dreams,
but I wasn't willing to give them up either —
that is, until now.

'For the first time I understood
what they meant,
what they were doing to my relationship
with the Lord.

In truth, I was an unfaithful wife,
reserving a part of my heart
for someone, or something, other than Him.
'Forgive me, O Lord,'
I prayed.
'I renounce everything but You.
I love You, and You alone,
with all of my heart.'

'There, in the pre-dawn darkness,
in that tiny bathroom,
with my tear-damp face pressed against
the rough-textured wall,
I made my peace with God,
the lover of my soul.
I walked from there
a new man,
never to dream that dream again
so long as God
was my heart's only desire."

I've only dreamed that dream one time since. For several years I hosted a live, ninety-minute, call-in radio broadcast on Sunday nights. It proved to be an effective vehicle for ministry, and the station manager asked me to host a daily program as well. After much discussion, I reluctantly agreed. When I shared my decision with the radio staff, they were apprehensive, but deferred to my judgment.

That very night I dreamed that dream again, only this time Brenda was emotionally involved with a preacher with a national ministry. He was not identified in my dream, but somehow I knew how successful and powerful he was. When I awoke, I knew instantly what God was telling me.

91

This radio opportunity was not part of His plan for my life. Once again I was tempted with wealth and power, only this time it was in the form of a "ministry"! Needless to say, I immediately called the station manager and told him that I couldn't accept his offer; God would not permit it.

Herein lies the subtlety of power — often it comes disguised as ministry, an opportunity to do something important for God. I shudder to think what might have happened if it had not been for the apprehension of my staff, the faithfulness of a friend to speak the truth in love, and that God-given dream.

The potential for the abuse of power is present in every one of us. Frequently, it is held in check, not by true humility, but only by a lack of opportunity. If we are given a little power, let the world beware! Alone, none of us is a match for its beguiling temptations, but together in mutual accountability, with God's help, we can overcome. Loving service, humble service, in a room where nobody sees and nobody knows, is what transforms power into redemptive ministry. Only in serving others are we saved from our selfish selves and from the perils of power.

Footnotes

[1]"A Year to Forget," *Christianity Today* (Mar. 18, 1988), p. 45.

[2]"The Fall of Jimmy Swaggart," *People Weekly* (Mar. 7, 1988), p. 37.

[3]"I Made Mistakes," *Christianity Today* (Mar. 18, 1988), p. 47.

[4]"Good News for the Disenfranchised," *Christianity Today* (Mar. 18, 1988), p. 33.

[5]Ibid., p. 33.

[6]Richard J. Foster, *Money, Sex & Power* (San Francisco: Harper & Row, Publishers, 1985), pp. 178-189.

[7]Foster, p. 223

[8]Foster, p. 240.

Chapter 5

REHABILITATION

AND RESTORATION

In recent months we have become reluctant witnesses to the moral indiscretions of some of Christianity's most visible spokesmen. The reactions of believers have varied from outright disbelief ("It's a lie of the enemy") to self-righteous judgment ("It's a disgrace and they shouldn't be allowed to preach ever again").

Thus far in this book we have dealt with the underlying causes of this kind of moral failure on the part of our spiritual leaders — lust, inappropriate relationships, mid-life frustrations, and the abuse of power. Both research and personal experience indicate that virtually all ministerial immorality is the result of one of these factors, or a combination thereof.

The question before us now is: how should the Church minister to these fallen brothers? Some have encouraged us to "forgive and forget," while others have counseled severe disciplinary action. Almost everyone has an opinion, but what does the Bible say?

Unfortunately the New Testament is strangely silent on this subject, perhaps because none of the early Church leaders fell into sexual sin — at least, none of the apostles. While that's a wonderful testimony, it does little to help us with our dilemma.

In Romans 16:17,18 Paul does warn us ". . . to watch out for those who cause divisions and put obstacles in your way that are contrary to the teaching you have learned." He then says, *"Keep away from them. For such people are not serving our Lord Christ, but their own appetites. By smooth talk and flattery they deceive the minds of naive people"* (Rom. 16:17,18). (emphasis mine)

Peter too warns about false teachers, immoral ministers, who, according to him, are bold and arrogant, despise authority and blaspheme in matters they do not understand. He writes:

"With eyes full of adultery, they never stop sinning; they seduce the unstable; they are experts in greed — an accursed brood! They have left the straight way and wandered off to follow the way of Balaam son of Beor, who loved the wages of wickedness . . . For they mouth empty, boastful words and, by appealing to the lustful desires of sinful human nature, they entice people who are just escaping from those who live in error. They promise them freedom, while they themselves are slaves of depravity . . . ."

2 Peter 2:14,15,18,19

I do not mean to imply, with these scriptures, that every minister who falls into sin is necessarily an enemy

94

of Christ who should be avoided. It is important, however, to note that the apostles took their high calling seriously, and they demanded the same from those who shared the ministry. If a person persisted in using the ministry for his own ends, they were quick to warn the Body and counseled them to cut that man off from Christian fellowship. The purpose in such action was twofold: 1) to preserve the Body, and 2) to discipline the erring minister. If he responded to the correction of the Church, he could be restored; but if he did not, then he would have to accept the consequences resulting from his own actions.

In 1 Corinthians 5:1,2, Paul addresses the issue of immorality in the Church and gives us some guidelines for dealing with it: "It is actually reported that there is sexual immorality among you, and of a kind that does not occur even among pagans: A man has his father's wife. *And you are proud!* Shouldn't you rather have been filled with grief and have put out of your fellowship the man who did this?" (emphasis mine)

Apparently Paul is dismayed by two things the man's blatant immorality, and the church's apparent indifference to it, even acceptance of it. Gordon Fee, professor of New Testament at Regent College and author of several books says: "It is this lack of a sense of sin, and therefore of any ethical consequences to their life in the Spirit, that marks the Corinthian brand of spirituality as radically different from that which flows out of the gospel of Christ crucified. And it is precisely this failure to recognize the depth of their *corporate sinfulness* due to their arrogance that causes Paul to take such strong action . . . ."[1] (emphasis mine)

What a striking commentary on the American Church. We too, in many ways, seem indifferent toward immorality, even in the ministry. We call our attitude "unconditional love," but it may well be closer to licentiousness. How little we seem to know of the grief our sinfulness causes Christ.

Early one Sunday morning, in July 1984, I entered my study to prepare my heart for the morning service. As I was sitting at my desk in prayer, I received a vision. In this vision I saw the Church in, what at first appeared to be, a large banquet hall. Believers were laughing and talking, eating and fellowshipping. I saw myself walking among them, from table to table. What I overheard was disturbing indeed. Their table talk was anything but what you would expect from the Body of Christ. There was little or no conversation relating to spiritual matters. Instead, there was foolish talk and coarse jesting, profanity, sexual innuendo, and suggestive stories.

Looking up, I saw Jesus standing in the foyer with a pained expression on His face. It was then I realized that this was no banquet hall, at least not in the ordinary sense, but a house of prostitution. Then I heard a new sound — worship? The church was worshipping. Yet it was strange, different. One moment they were laughing and jesting profanely, and the next they were speaking in tongues and prophesying. It was both disconcerting and encouraging, and I rushed to tell Jesus that things weren't as bad as they might appear.

As soon as I reached Him I said, "Jesus, I know that things look bad but I have heard them worshipping, praying, even prophesying in Your name."

Without a word, He grabbed His stomach and doubled over. Then He began to weep, great groaning sobs racked

His body. Only then did I realize that it was worse than I had thought. Instead of being comforted by the fact that His people were manifesting spiritual gifts, even as they sat in a house of prostitution, He was heartbroken. The vision faded and I was left sitting at my desk, alone, weeping, under great conviction.

Four years ago I had no idea what that vision meant, at least no idea concerning its scope. I assumed it was for me and my church, and it was. God was calling us to repentance and true holiness. But it was broader than that, it was for the whole Body of Christ. It was a prophetic vision about sexual sin in the Body.

Now, in retrospect, how obvious that seems. In truth, for all of our spiritual manifestations we were living in sin, in a house of prostitution.

> Then it seemed that the Lord spoke to me:
> " 'From the least to the greatest,
>   all are greedy for gain;
> prophets and priests alike,
>   all practice deceit.
> *They dress the wound of my people*
>   *as though it were not serious.*
> "Peace, peace," they say,
>   when there is no peace.
> Are they ashamed of their loathsome
>   conduct?
>   No, *they have no shame at all;*
>   *they do not even know how to*
>   *blush.*
> So they will fall among the fallen;
>   they will be brought down when I
>   punish them,'
>   says the Lord.

" '. . . I am bringing disaster on this people,
   the fruit of their schemes,
because they have not listened to my
      words,
   and have rejected my law.' "

Jeremiah 6:13-15,19 (emphasis mine)

In light of that passage from Jeremiah, it would seem that God is as grieved by our nonchalant attitude toward sin as He is by the actual sin itself. To be sure, immorality in the ministry is no small thing, but neither is the almost prideful way we congratulate ourselves for being "unconditional" in our love and forgiveness. " 'Are . . . (we) . . . ashamed of their loathsome conduct? No, . . . (we) . . . have no shame at all; . . . (we) . . . do not even know how to blush . . .' " (Jer. 6:15). Perhaps we need to read again Paul's words to the church in Corinth, ". . . Shouldn't you rather have been *filled with grief* . . .?" (1 Cor. 5:2). (emphasis mine)

Apparently this Corinthian man's sin was common knowledge, and he seemed intent on continuing his incestuous relationship. To complicate matters even further, he had no intention of removing himself from the church. In that case Paul instructed the believers in Corinth:

"When you are assembled in the name of our Lord Jesus and I am with you in spirit, and the power of our Lord Jesus is present, hand this man over to Satan, so that the sinful nature may be destroyed and his spirit saved on the day of the Lord . . . . *you must not associate with anyone who calls himself a brother but is sexually immoral* or greedy, an idolater or a slanderer, a drunkard or a swindler. With such a man do not even eat." (emphasis mine)

1 Corinthians 5:4,5,11

Please note that ex-communication was reserved for the impenitent, and was a last resort, to be employed only when all else fails. Even then its goal is redemptive, not punitive.

This man's sin was public knowledge, therefore his discipline was also public. Paul instructs young Timothy regarding the discipline of elders (spiritual leaders): "Those who sin are to be rebuked publicly, so that the others may take warning" (1 Tim. 5:20). Notice I use the word *discipline* and not *punishment*. Punishment focuses on past mistakes, while discipline focuses on correct future behavior. The Church's intent was not to rid themselves of an undesirable brother, but to be the instrument of God in his ultimate redemption — ". . . that the sinful nature may be destroyed and his spirit saved . . . ." (1 Cor. 5:5).

The attitude or "spirit" of the disciplining body is of critical importance. They must not be angry, but grieved: ". . . Shouldn't you rather have been filled with grief . . .?" (1 Cor. 5:2). They must be firm, but meek; not in any way self-righteous or superior. Paul says, ". . . do not regard him as an enemy, but warn him as a brother" (2 Thess. 3:15). If that warning does not produce true repentance, then additional action must be taken. ". . . Expel the wicked man from among you," (1 Cor. 5:13) commands the apostle. In his commentary on First Corinthians, Gordon Fee writes: "There are always some who see this action as harsh and unloving; but such criticism comes from those who do not appreciate the biblical view of God's holiness, and the deep revulsion to sin that that holiness entails."[2]

In addition to serving as an instrument in the redemption of a fallen brother, such discipline also preserves the integrity of the Body. Notice I did not say the reputation of the Body, but its integrity. Paul says, ". . . Don't you know that a little yeast works through the whole batch of dough? Get rid of the old yeast that you may be a new batch without yeast . . . bread without yeast, the bread of sincerity and truth" (1 Cor. 5:6-8).

What does all of this have to do with the minister who sins sexually, especially if he confesses after his secret sin is discovered? Considerable, I believe. First, it means that we have a spiritual responsibility, both to the body of believers, and to him. Discipline is mandatory. Without it the sinful nature will not be destroyed. What form that discipline should take is not spelled out in scripture, but that it is necessary is quite clear. We must become the instrument of God for the redemption and restoration of our fallen brother. A period of suspension, when the minister is not permitted to preach, followed by a probationary period, is not punishment, but redemptive discipline which allows the Holy Spirit to complete His healing work.

Let me say it again: suspension and probation are disciplines designed for the restoration of the penitent and should not be confused with ex-communication which is reserved for the impenitent.

Some may contend that the man in First Corinthians 5 was not a minister and therefore his case should not be used as a model. A point well taken, but let me remind you that in the New Testament Church there was no formal distinction between the clergy and the laity. All were called to serve (Rom. 1:6), all were gifted for ministry (Rom. 12:5-8; 1 Cor. 12:4-11), and all were part of the holy priesthood of believers. (1 Pet. 2:9). Therefore, any principles regarding the discipline of a member of the Body would apply also to the discipline of the "minister." If an "ordinary" believer was disciplined this severely, then how much more severe would the discipline be for one in a position of greater spiritual responsibility.

When the infidelity of a minister comes to light, we want to assume the best; we want to believe that it was something that happened only once, in a moment of weakness. Unfortunately, that is usually not the case. Instead, we often discover that it has been a tragic pattern for a number of months, perhaps even years. Frequently it has involved several different women.

I mention all of that only to help us better understand the depth of the problem and the desperate need the minister has for a period of time, away from the ministry, when he can deal with the destructive habits of a lifetime. Even when a minister confesses and repents, it is still in his best interest to require him to cease ministering for a time in order to rearrange his priorities and re-establish his family relationships.

Adultery is seldom just a "sexual sin," and while it is definitely a spiritual problem, it is more than just a "spiritual problem." It involves a number of factors including, but not limited to, the way we relate to our spouse, our own self-image and sexual identity, our lifestyle, our work habits, and even the way we do ministry. These are issues which simply cannot be dealt with in a brief encounter, or in a few days away, nor can they be adequately addressed while the minister is still involved full time in ministry. The pressures of ministry are simply too great, the temptation to return to the familiar routine too compelling — a routine which contributed significantly to the problem in the first place.

No, in order to be fully restored, the minister must remove himself from ministry for a time.

At first, suspension and probation may seem harsh, even vindictive, but let me remind you that according to the survey conducted by *Leadership,*[3] only 4 per cent of ministers involved in moral indiscretion were ever found out. What's the point? Simply this: In His great mercy, God apparently gives ministers considerable space to repent, to "work out their own salvation," as it were, before He allows their sin to be exposed publicly. If that is true (and I believe it generally is), then by the time it does become public knowledge it has been a deeply rooted habit for a considerable length of time, perhaps even years.

A recent article in *Leadership* (Winter Quarter, 1988) is a case in point. It was written by the wife of a minister who was guilty of repeated affairs spanning several years, a fact he kept well covered for over fourteen years:

". . . it took six days of confrontation to extract all the facts. Through clever hedging and conscious lying, Bill had covered the extent of his immoral actions.

"These are facts I still struggle with today: Fourteen years ago he was confronted by an attractive woman in our small church, who stated that she planned to leave the church because she was in love with him. Subsequently she invited him to join her at a motel where she had gone for 'a day of seeking God's will.' That affair lasted six months. They cut it off, knowing they were not meant to live together. She was my friend before, during, and after.

"There were ten years free of involvement until one of the women who later signed a statement against Bill chased him until she caught him. I knew she was chasing, but I assumed he was running.

"A few other involvements of varying degrees followed in a short period of time. He set them all aside for a year, and then we moved to another church.

"In time he entered a low-level affair, which lasted three months until just prior to the confrontations (with the new pastor of our former church and the district superintendent who had signed statements charging Bill with inappropriate behavior and immoral actions)."[4]

Bill and countless others like him are not evil men, in fact they often love God deeply and give themselves sacrificially to the ministry. Unfortunately, an inadvertent slip, in a moment of weakness, becomes a lifestyle, which in turn becomes bondage. Paul puts it this way: "Know ye not, that to whom ye yield yourselves servants to obey, his servants ye are . . .?" (Rom. 6:16 KJV).

In order to break this sinful pattern, offenders will usually require outside help and a drastic change of scenery. Yet what minister will dare risk acknowledging his need to another, when to do so is to risk having his sin made known to his wife, his brethren, and quite possibly his church? The risk simply seems too great. Instead, he struggles in secret until that tragic day when his sin is exposed for all the world to see.

Observing him then, in the pain and humility of his brokenness, it would be easy to allow our sympathy to blind us to his deeper need for healing and true restoration. If he is to be saved, then we must render redemptive discipline out of a heart of true compassion. We must do for him what he is incapable of doing for himself — we must remove him from ministry for a time so he may be fully restored in all the relationships of his life. An understanding of these spiritual and emotional dynamics makes accountability mandatory. And there can be no accountability unless the ones to whom we are accountable have the authority to decide and enforce discipline.

Following the recent revelations of Jimmy Swaggart's sexual indiscretions, much ado was made about judging him. It was suggested that the Assemblies of God had better be very careful, and that only Jimmy Swaggart could decide when he should return to the pulpit. Such remarks seemed to me to display a remarkable ignorance regarding the whole subject of authority and accountability.

In 1 Corinthians 5:12,13 Paul says: "What business is it of mine to judge those outside the church? *Are you not to judge those inside?* God will judge those outside. 'Expel the wicked man from among you.' " (emphasis mine) From this passage it is clear that the Church has not only the right, but the responsibility, to judge its own members. Let it be noted that the scriptures are not talking about judging petty matters of personal conviction.* The kind of church discipline mentioned here is reserved for matters that are clearly defined in the scriptures as sin.

---

*Jesus talks about that kind of judging in Matthew 7:1,3-5 and says: " 'Do not judge, or you too will be judged . . . . Why do you look at the speck of sawdust in your brother's eye and pay no attention to the plank in your own eye. How can you say to your brother, 'Let me take the speck out of your eye,' when all the time there is a plank in your own eye? You hypocrite, first take the plank out of your own eye, and then you will see clearly to remove the speck from your brother's eye.' "

104

Additionally, it should be noted that this kind of action passes judgment on a person's behavior rather than on the person himself. The person is still eternally valuable, to God and to the Church. In fact, the goal of our judgment is redemptive, not punitive. It makes a statement regarding both his personhood and his behavior. It says that he is loved unconditionally, but that his lifestyle is unacceptable; and until his behavior changes, we will love him, but we will not fellowship with him.

In order to be the instrument of God, for redemption and healing, the Church must recognize the difference between unconditional love and unconditional fellowship. We have often confused the two, and in so doing, we have created a climate of permissiveness which is neither loving nor redemptive.

God loves us unconditionally; that is, there is nothing we can do to make Him love us less — no evil act, no immorality, no gross sin, nothing! His love is a manifestation of Who He is, and is not dependent, in any way, on our behavior. It's the expression of His nature and character. We are merely the objects of His eternal love. But for all of that, He will not fellowship with us unconditionally:

". . . God is light; in him there is no darkness at all. If we claim to have fellowship with him yet walk in the darkness, we lie and do not live by the truth. But if we walk in the light, as he is in the light, we have fellowship with one another, and the blood of Jesus, his Son, purifies us from every sin."

1 John 1:5-7

God says, "No matter what you do, I will love you. No matter where you go, I will love you. No matter how far you wander, or how low you sink, I will love you! Yet, even though I love you totally, eternally, unconditionally, I will not fellowship with you unless you walk in the light."

God's model: unconditional love, conditional fellowship. In order to experience the benefits of His great love, we must fellowship with Him, and in order to fellowship with Him we must walk in the light as He is in the light.

When the Church disciplines a fallen minister, it is simply enforcing this principle. We love him, but his behavior has made it impossible for us to fellowship with him. We must not do anything, in word or in deed, that would lead him to believe that his sinful behavior is acceptable, either to us, or to God. We love him too much to allow him to continue, unchecked, in his self-destructive behavior. ". . . Do not associate with him," writes Paul, "in order that he may feel ashamed. Yet do not regard him as an enemy, but warn him as a brother" (2 Thess. 3:14,15).

Once the Church has exercised its God-given responsibility, then the burden of action falls upon the minister. Will he respond in humility and repentance? Will he submit himself to the authority of the Church? Will he endure the painful rigors of God's discipline? Or will he opt for an easier way? Sometimes the Lord's discipline, expressed through His Church, seems harsh and unforgiving, but it is not.

> ". . . 'My son, do not make light of the
>   Lord's discipline,
> and do not lose heart when he
>   rebukes you,
> because the Lord disciplines those he
>   loves . . . .'

"No discipline seems pleasant at the time, but painful. Later on, however, it produces a harvest of righteousness and peace for those who have been trained by it."

Hebrews 12:5,6,11

The Apostle Paul has established, not only the Church's responsibility to judge its membership (ministers included), but also its authority. In fact, its very right to judge implies its authority, for without authority it could not judge. In Romans 13:1-5 he writes:

"Everyone must submit himself to the governing authorities, *for there is no authority except that which God has established. The authorities that exist have been established by God.* Consequently, he who rebels against the authority is rebelling against what God has instituted, and those who do so will bring judgment on themselves. For rulers hold no terror for those who do right, but for those who do wrong. Do you want to be free from fear of the one in authority? Then do what is right and he will commend you. For he is God's servant to do you good. But if you do wrong, be afraid, for he does not bear the sword for nothing. He is God's servant, an agent of wrath to bring punishment on the wrongdoer. Therefore it is necessary to submit to the authorities, not only because of possible punishment but also because of conscience." (emphasis mine)

If, as Paul so eloquently contends, even the civil authorities have been established by God, then how much more can we be sure that God has also established the ecclesiastical authorities. Does it not stand to reason then that the minister who rejects the discipline of the Church is rejecting the authority God has set up? ". . . and those who do so," reasons Paul, "will bring judgment on

107

themselves" (v. 2). In light of scripture, I think it behooves the minister, who is under discipline, to accept the decision of the Church,* and to submit himself to its rehabilitation in order that he may be restored.

While we are on the subject of accountability, let me say that it has two sides — discipline and responsibility. When the Church holds its ministers accountable and accepts the authority to mete out discipline, it is also charged, by God, with the responsibility for their spiritual care. For the most part the Church has been fairly responsible in the area of discipline; however, when it comes to spiritual care for its ministers, it has been sadly lacking.

To a significant degree pastors are responsible for developing their own spiritual resources. Little spiritual care is provided for them beyond some token functions, which usually follow a conference format, providing little or no opportunity for in-depth personal ministry. Should a personal crisis develop, the district officials are usually available for counsel and support, but that is often too little too late.

These observations are not intended to discredit the district officials who frequently are stretched far too thin. By both their job description, and the demands of their office, they are required to spend much of their time in administration and trouble shooting. Their work load is demanding, their hours long, and their duties often make

---

*There are instances when the committed believer must obey God rather than man, but those situations involve matters of spiritual principle rather than personal sin. For instance, it was a matter of spiritual truth which motivated Martin Luther to challenge the Catholic Church and nail his ninety-five theses to the door. In much the same way, Dietrich Bonhoeffer and pastor Martin Niemoller both challenged the evil government of the Nazis. In neither case were their actions motivated by self-interest.

it necessary for them to travel hundreds of miles every week. Unfortunately, much of their efforts are devoted to details, troubled churches or disciplinary action, leaving almost no time or energy for positive spiritual care.

As pastors we face the same difficulty in our churches. It seems we never have enough time to take care of everything so we end up taking care of details and emergencies. Is there an answer, a solution? Yes! Some churches are addressing this problem by equipping the laity to provide pastoral care. The actual ministry itself is accomplished through home fellowship groups, lay counseling centers, spiritual growth groups, retreats and the informal fellowship that is such a vital dynamic of the true Church.

Perhaps something along this line could be incorporated, at the district or conference level, with the emphasis on relationships rather than activities. Local pastors could be trained to serve as group facilitators. The emphasis would be ministry and spiritual care rather than church business. For maximum benefit the groups would need to be small, consisting of not more than twelve or fifteen ministers. They would need a covenant relationship, including a commitment to attendance, daily prayer for one another, and confidentiality. In such a relationship spiritual problems and temptations could be identified and dealt with before they became "major" sins, thus preventing some of the tragedies which have necessitated a book such as this.

Dietrich Bonhoeffer, the German theologian and martyr, wrote:

"*He who is alone with his sin is utterly alone.* It may be that Christians, notwithstanding corporate worship, common prayer, and all their fellowship in service, may still be left to their loneliness. The final break-through does not occur, because, though they have fellowship with one another as believers and as devout people, they do not have fellowship as the undevout, as sinners. *The pious fellowship permits no one to be a sinner. So everyone must conceal his sin from himself and from the fellowship.* We dare not be sinners. Many Christians are unthinkably horrified when a real sinner is suddenly discovered among the righteous. So *we remain alone with our sin, living in lies and hypocrisy.* The fact is that we are sinners."[5] (emphasis mine)

Bonhoeffer has touched a nerve, hasn't he? "The pious fellowship permits no one to be a sinner. So everyone must conceal his sin from himself and from the fellowship . . . . So we remain alone with our sin, living in lies and hypocrisy."

Herein lies the tragedy. The Church has supposed that it could make us holy by pretending we were without sin. Instead it has made us hypocrites. Freedom from sin does not come through denying our sinfulness, but in confessing it to each other and to God. In the transparent fellowship, sin is deprived of both its strength and its power. Its strength is its secrecy. As long as it is not exposed to the power of true Christian fellowship it can continue to dominate us, but once it's exposed to the light, its hold is broken. Sin's power is its ability to isolate us from the fellowship, to make us feel that we are the only person who has ever been tempted this way. Alone we are no match for its subtle temptations, but together with the fellowship we can defeat it.

Which brings up another point — confidential rehabilitation. The need exists, I believe, for a means whereby a minister can voluntarily confess his sin without fear of exposure or recrimination. If such a forum existed, in conjunction with true spiritual care, I believe many ministers could be delivered from immorality before it became a lifestyle. I see no scriptural reason why a minister's indiscretion need be made public if he has forsaken his sin, voluntarily confessed, submitted to the proper authorities for rehabilitation, and the sin has not become public knowledge. Paul says: "Brothers, if someone is caught in a sin, you who are spiritual should restore him gently. But watch yourself, or you also may be tempted" (Gal. 6:1).

Complicating the whole disciplinary process are the financial concerns of the minister and his family. Heather Bryce writes in *After the Affair: A Wife's Story:* "Soon, if not immediately, my husband would have no ministry — maybe anywhere, ever. We would have to leave our parsonage and our church family. All security was gone . . . . Pastors don't receive unemployment, and paychecks cease. And no entry-level job can replace the salary of a senior pastor after twenty-five years of ministry."[6]

In their case, a number of concerned friends took up a collection so they could spend some weeks in a retreat center for clergy couples in crisis, and eventually Bill took a job in sales. Still, that is so little in light of the traumatic needs of the minister and his family.

If indeed, the Church is serious about rehabilitating its ministers (and I believe it is), then it must take some significant action to provide formal counseling, in a spiritual setting, designed for the unique needs of the minister and his spouse. It must also set aside funds, not only to underwrite the cost of the counseling center, but also to provide living expenses for the minister's family while he is receiving treatment.

I realize that these are ambitious recommendations, but the magnitude of the problem, not to mention the eternal consequences, demands aggressive action.

Footnotes

[1]Gordon D. Fee, "The First Epistle To The Corinthians," *The New International Commentary On The New Testament* (Grand Rapids: William B. Eerdmans Publishing Company, 1987), p. 203.

[2]Ibid.

[3]"How Common Is Pastoral Indiscretion?" *Leadership* (Winter Quarter, 1988), p. 13.

[4]Heather Bryce (a pen name), "After the Affair: A Wife's Story," *Leadership* (Winter Quarter, 1988) p. 60.

[5]Dietrich Bonhoeffer, "Life Together," quoted in *Disciplines for the Inner Life* by Bob Benson and Michael W. Benson (Waco: Word Books Publisher, 1985), pp. 55,60.

[6]Bryce, pp. 59,63.

Chapter 6

RESTORING

THE MARRIAGE

She had come for healing prayer and now she stood before me wheezing, fighting painfully for each breath. We prayed, but with no visible results. A second time. And then a third time. Still there was no relief. Finally, I asked her if we could talk. She nodded a reply, and we made our way to the end of the altar and sat down.

"How long have you been troubled with asthma?" I asked.

"About four years," she said, "maybe four and a half."

"Are you telling me that you never had a single asthmatic attack until four years ago?"

She nodded.

"What about during your childhood?" I pressed. "Surely there were times while you were growing up."

"Never!"

I tried another tack. "What was going on in your life four or five years ago?"

She winched visibly, and fought to control her emotions, wheezing noisily all the while. Finally she spoke, in a hoarse whisper, hardly loud enough to be heard, but with an awful intensity.

Her story was painfully real, and far too familiar. About ten years earlier she and her husband had pioneered a church. For a while things seemed to go pretty well, then the trouble started. Over nothing really, but once it got started there was no stopping it. The criticism was vicious. People they had thought were their friends turned on them, told lies, campaigned to have them removed from the church. Finally the church spilt. Things seemed to settle down after that, but her husband had never recovered.

A few months later she discovered that he was having an affair with her best friend. For a while she had lived with that terrible secret, afraid to confront him, hoping that it would run its course, that he would come to his senses. Then the rumors started, and the phone calls from concerned "friends," telling her that they had been seen together, her husband and her best friend. Finally, she confronted him, and her worst fears were realized. He resigned the church, left the ministry, filed for a divorce and married her friend. She was left alone, facing fifty, without a hope in the world.

As she talked I realized that this was the other side of ministerial adultery — the experience of the betrayed spouse. Although ministerial infidelity usually doesn't end in divorce, the betrayed wife still experiences many of these same emotions, terrible and terrifying. She's angry with him: how could he do such a thing? And she's angry with "her," the other woman: has she no shame? And she's angry with God! How could He let such a thing happen? Hatred boils inside of her like a thing alive, bitter and vile, seeking revenge. And as incongruent as it may seem, she feels guilty, as if it were somehow her fault.

Then there's the pain. Constantly she finds herself rubbing something: her temples because of a headache, her stomach as though with indigestion, her eyes for lack of sleep. She feels humiliated, rejected. "And if that adultery indeed 'didn't mean anything to (him),' as (her) spouse may suggest, then the lovemaking of (their) own marriage was sold for a mess of pottage. Its value is meaningless if it can be betrayed for a meaningless moment of sexual pleasure. That is personal. That is humiliating."[1] And finally there is confusion. She walks around as if she is in a fog. Her security is gone, her whole world has gone off-center, she has no idea what the future holds.

Following the discovery of her husband's adultery, one pastor's wife said: " it felt like every point, every security, everything in my life that had brought me happiness had been reduced to nothingness. I felt like someone had taken out my heart, tramped it, smashed it, beat it with a sledgehammer, and put it back inside this body. It still beats, but it beats a little crooked."[2]

Another writes: "The next two days, I moved in slow motion. It was hard to talk. Even lifting a fork took effort . . . . I wandered through our parsonage, trying to visualize packing and moving out. I couldn't. I couldn't cope with the thought.

"At night I began waking often. I'd try to understand my new situation. *I'm married to a man I don't know. I'm not a pastor's wife anymore.*"³ (emphasis mine)

Imagine how she feels. This isn't the man she married; that man was good and godly, incapable of the kind of things this man has done. Unspeakable things, sinful things, things beyond the realm of her comprehension. And not only has he done them, but he has confessed them to her in sordid detail. She trusted him, never thought to question his late hours. She believed him when he told her his preoccupation was church-related, pastoral pressure; but now her trust is gone, crushed beneath the awful fact of his unfaithfulness.

Yet she wants to save their marriage; she wants to forgive him as badly as he wants to be forgiven; but can she? Can she get rid of her hurt and anger without destroying him, them? Can she learn to trust him again, respect him as a godly man, as the spiritual leader in their home? These and a hundred more questions haunt her every waking moment.

He too is tormented. And, in a sense, he is relieved, freed finally, of living with his terrible secret, done with his double life. Yet at what a dreadful cost. In telling the truth, he has destroyed his own self-image. No longer can he pretend that he is what he appeared to be — a godly man of spiritual and moral integrity. Somehow, for years, he has managed to live a lie — but no more. Now everyone knows, now everywhere he turns he is brought face to face with his shameful failure. His confession has destroyed the faith placed in him by his peers, his trusting congregation, his family. It is almost more than he can bear.

One pastor described his experience this way:

"Somehow I made it through the public confession, on adrenalin I think, but following the benediction an awful weariness settled upon me. Like a sleep walker I made my way down the center aisle to the front doors. Years of weekly repetition gave my handshake firmness, my smile a warmth I didn't feel, and my words a personableness which belied the awful emptiness within. Eventually the last worshipper departed and I re-entered the now empty sanctuary and looked around in despair. The silence was overwhelming, almost erie. I made my way to the altar, then to the pulpit.

"Standing there it all came back — my call to the ministry, the skimpy years when we both had to work so I could finish seminary, my first sermon, the night I was ordained, our first church. Then I begin to weep, soundlessly at first, just huge tears running down my cheeks, then harder until my whole body shook. Great heaving sobs rent my soul. I wept for what might have been, what should have been. I cried for my wife, for the terrible pain I had caused her, for the anguish that now locked her in painful silence. I cried for my church. They deserved better than this. They had trusted me, loved me, and I betrayed them. And I cried for me, for the man I might have been.

"I stood behind the pulpit, touched it, ran my fingers over the smooth wood and realized as never before what a sacred place it was. And with that realization came guilt so great that I couldn't breath. The magnitude of my sin, my betrayal, drove me from the pulpit and I stumbled to the altar and sat down. An accusing voice inside of me whispered, 'How are the mighty fallen.'

"There was no reason to stay, no reason to linger longer, but I couldn't tear myself away. My life was ending, unraveling thread by thread, and I was powerless to stop

117

it. Over the years, I had told ministers, again and again, that they had identity as persons not just as preachers, but now I discovered it wasn't true for me. Without the pulpit, the church, the ministry, I had no self. I could feel myself becoming invisible, turning into a nonentity — breathing and taking up space but having absolutely no reason to exist."

Now adultery is tragic for anyone, but as Heather Bryce points out, "The average parishioner who falls need only come to the pastor's office with his or her spouse, confess, and receive forgiveness. The two are given support and go on with their lives. The situation is painful, but few know. The couple keep their jobs, home, and sense of community.

"A pastor who confesses, on the other hand, usually loses his position and income and residence, and is forced to leave the very community that should be giving him emotional support. He will be asked to confess publicly. He must resign all hard-won places of honor with his peers and denomination.

"The bewildered, stunned pastor's wife suffers losses in addition to her husband's. They will move, thus costing her contact with her friends, and she may well lose her husband. *At the least, she has lost her pastor.* She loses her self-worth from both the adulteries and from losing the ministries where she received approval. Since few people understand the whole situation, she is isolated at her point of greatest need. When able to stay within the marriage relationship her only companion is the one who acted to her hurt."[4] (emphasis mine) Her past, once cherished is gone. She loathes and is contaminated by it.

It is surely obvious by now that a moral failure in the ministry is a complex issue creating a host of genuine concerns. The ministry of restoration must attempt to address them all — the spiritual life of the minister, the minister's marriage, his ministry, and, of course, the spiritual life of the church. The question before us now is: can the minister's broken marriage be restored? If so, how?

First, there must be honest confession and true repentance. This will not be easy, for the truth of infidelity is terribly painful. The adulterer has deceived himself, has developed an elaborate system of rationalization whereby he is able to explain, to himself, his unexplainable behavior. In confession he experiences, maybe for the first time, the true magnitude of his sin. He suddenly sees himself through his wife's eyes. He is a liar and a deceiver. His immorality has made a mockery out of his faith and his marriage. In the terrible pain of that moment he will be tempted to withhold some of the details. He will probably attempt to explain, to justify, his actions. While this is understandable, it only delays the healing process.

He may attempt to avoid the full disclosure of his shameful deeds in order to spare his wife's feelings. A noble thought, but inappropriate now. Any further dishonesty will only wound her deeper. In order for this marriage to live again, it must die; that is, the false marriage that was built upon lies and broken vows must die. There can be no more half-truths, no more pretending.

Wangerin says: ". . . in hiding the deed, he hides something of himself from the marriage, something of his real being — an adultery, either brief or lasting, is always evidence of an attitude, the quality of the adulterer's soul. He hides his personal tendencies, his view of this marriage,

119

his needs or weaknesses, his character. The marriage cannot be whole when something so essential has been amputated from it."[5]

The adulterer may reason that if his wife knows the extent of his unfaithfulness, how many years it has lasted, how many different women it has involved, how elaborate his deceit, she may not be able to bear it. His concern is well justified. In truth, she may not be able to bear it; the marriage may be destroyed by the terrible truth of his sin. Still, it is the only way. For certain any further dishonesty will be terminal for the marriage. By now she has a nose for the truth. No longer is she willing to discount her instinct as foolish jealousy. The thing she knew, but refused to believe, has proven true. Now she will not stop until she has the full truth, she will follow her instincts, she will fight her way through his weak lies, she must know the truth no matter how painful!

It probably won't all come out at once. He simply does not have the stomach for it; it is more than he can bear, more than he can admit to himself. Over a few days, perhaps as much as two to three weeks, he will finally tell all. It will be a traumatic time for both the minister and his wife, with wide swings of emotion ranging from almost uncontrollable rage to numbing grief. The help of a Christian counselor is invaluable during this period and in the reconstruction of the marriage which is to follow. Few couples have the resources to rebuild their marriage without competent assistance, therefore they must be encouraged to seek help.

Once a wife knows the truth of her husband's adultery, she will have to process her feelings. The presence of a compassionate Christian counselor is almost mandatory during this process. He serves as both a nonjudgmental listener and a spiritual facilitator. He holds the betrayed spouse accountable, helps her deal with the hurts and anger she might otherwise bury, for he knows that anger and bitterness must be acknowledged and confessed before forgiveness can be extended to the offending spouse.

Before she can forgive her spouse for his failures, his adulteries, she must confess her anger to God. That is, she must relive the hurtful incidents in the presence of God. She must describe what has happened in complete and accurate detail and honestly confess her feelings. In truth, she feels them all over again and expresses them completely to the Lord.

At this stage she faces two dangers: On the one hand, she will be tempted to pass over this whole painful process. She does not want to remember it, does not want to relive the feelings all over again. She wants to hurry on to forgiveness, wants to put this entire sordid episode behind her. But if she does, those unfinished feelings will negate her forgiveness and undermine the marriage she wants to restore. On the other hand, she must be careful not to get stuck here. If she does not release those feelings and pronounce forgiveness, then her work has been in vain, she has not resolved her negative feelings, just recycled them.

The act of forgiveness itself is not unlike working through her painful emotions. Once again she must remember each and every hurtful incident, only this time the focus is different. Previously she embraced each painful memory, gave free vent to her emotions, full expression to her most violent grief. Now she releases both the memories and the emotions which accompany them. One by one, specifically, she forgives his lies, his deceit, his adulteries, everything. *This does not change the past, does not change what has happened; but it does something far more wonderful, it changes her!* Forgiveness is not a miracle that suddenly eradicates all her past hurts; but it is a miracle in the sense that it begins the slow healing process. It gives her the strength and the grace to forget the past and begin again.

Now she must confront her spouse with the truth of what his adulteries have done to her. He must be made to know everything she has suffered, everything she was made to feel. This is different from confessing her feelings to God. Then she was working through her feelings, pouring them out, as it were, but the object of her wrath was not present, so no one was hurt. This time she is confronting him, the object of her wrath, with the facts of his behavior. Her purpose is not to wound him — though he cannot truly repent until he feels her pain, and God's — but to confront him with the tragic truth of his sinful deeds. He must be made to know the awful sinfulness of his adultery. As long as he can explain it away, justify it in any way, there is no hope for him. His hope, his salvation, his very life, depends on his recognition of his sin, for only then can he truly repent.

Everything has to be bared, exposed to the light, in order for healing and trust to begin. Since God's forgiveness follows true repentance after full confession, there can be no hope for the future until every involvement is identified as sin, owned as his personal sin, and uprooted. Only then will sin wither and die!

Now it is time to get down to the real "grunt work" of rebuilding the marriage. Up to now there has been a lot of emotional highs and lows. Most likely the couple has spent some time in a counseling center, away from the press of day-to-day living, free from the demands of the ministry. There they have worked through many of the most volatile issues, but now the time has come for them to return to the real world. He will probably have to seek employment outside of the ministry for a while. She may have to return to the work force in order to make ends meet. Without question the rebuilding of their marriage will be done under enormous stress. The love and support of their ministerial colleagues is absolutely critical now.

Of primary importance is the rebuilding of trust, for without it marriage is hardly more than physical accommodation. Under the best of conditions trust is built slowly over an extended period of time. To rebuild it now will require not only time but a concentrated effort on the part of both spouses — but especially on his part.

Dr. Richard Dobbins, founder and director of Emerge Ministries, says:

"When an adulterous relationship has broken that bridge of trust, then building it back again frequently requires a healing period ranging from six months to two years . . . (the adulterous spouse) must realize that his infidelity has given his mate just cause to be both jealous and suspicious . . . . The mate who breaks the trust should volunteer information required for the mate whose trust has been shaken to check up on his whereabouts. Discovering that he is in the place he is supposed to be, doing what he said he would be doing, will help to rebuild that trust."[6]

In addition to that kind of accountability, there must be a re-bonding in their relationship. Intimacy (trust) in marriage is seldom possible unless a proper bonding has occurred between a husband and wife. Bonding refers to the emotional covenant that links a man and woman together for life. It is the "specialness" which sets those two lovers apart from every other person on the face of the earth.

According to Dr. Desmond Morris, author of *Intimate Behavior,* bonding is most likely to develop when a couple has moved systematically and slowly through twelve steps during their courtship and early marriage. Adultery breaks that bond by destroying trust and intimacy. It has been my experience that re-bonding can only occur by returning to the process which initially nurtured it — namely the twelve steps to close personal contact suggested by Dr. Morris:

"1. **Eye to body.** The most common form of social 'contact' is to look at people from a distance.

"2. **Eye to eye.** While we view others, they view us. If, then, one finds the other attractive, he or she may add a slight smile to the next meeting of the glances. If the response is returned, so is the smile, and further, more intimate contact may ensue.

"3. **Voice to voice.** Invariably the initial comments will contain concern trivia. This small-talk permits the reception of a further set of signals, this time to the ear instead of the eye.

"4. **Hand to hand.** The first actual body contact to occur is likely to be disguised as an act of 'supporting aid,' 'body protection' or 'directional guidance.' Only when the growing relationship has been openly declared will the action of hand-holding or arm-holding become prolonged in duration. It then ceases to be a 'supportive' or 'guiding' act and becomes an undisguised intimacy.

"5. **Arm to shoulder.** Up to this point the bodies have not come into close contact. When they do so, another important threshold has been passed. Walking together in this posture can be given the air of slight ambiguity, half way between close friendship and love.

"6. **Arm to waist.** This is something the man will not have done to other men, no matter how friendly, so that it becomes more of a direct statement of amorous intimacy.

"7. **Mouth to mouth.** Kissing on the mouth, combined with the full frontal embrace, is a major step forward.

"8. **Hand to head.** As an extension of the last stage, the hands begin to caress the partner's head. Fingers stroke the face, neck and hair. Hands clasp the nape and the side of the head."[7]

"9-12. **The final steps.** The last four levels of involvement are distinctly sexual and private . . . ."[8] (paraphrased)

Obviously, the final acts of physical contact should be reserved for the marital relationship, since they are progressively sexual and intensely personal.

Dr. James Dobson says: "The most successful marriages are those wherein husbands and wives journey through the twelve steps regularly in their daily lives. Touching and talking and holding hands and gazing into one another's eyes and building memories are as important to partners in their mid-life years as to rambunctious twenty-year-olds. Indeed, the best way to invigorate a tired sex life is to walk through the twelve steps of courtship, regularly and with gusto!"[9] And, I might add, it is critical to the re-bonding of the couple whose marriage has been shattered by infidelity.

Trust grows out of relationship, and the very heart of relationship is communication. Therefore it is vitally important that the recovering couple spend time together, getting to know each other again. Remember, honest and deep sharing takes time and effort. It doesn't just happen. You have to plan for it and give it priority.

Many couples have trouble communicating because they are too self-centered. This is particularly true of ministers and their wives. By the very nature of their work they are used to being the center of attention. Add the emotionally exhausting aspects of their people-centered ministry, and it is not hard to see why their communications break down. H. Norman Wright, Christian psychologist and marriage counselor, says: "As long as a person is preoccupied primarily with being understood by his spouse, he is miserable, overcome with self-pity, the spirit of demanding, and bitter withdrawal."[10]

If this marriage is to be fully restored, then each spouse must make a commitment to understand the other. She must realize that as a minister he faces not only unusual stress but special temptations as well. While he is ultimately responsible for the way he handles the unique demands of the ministry, she now realizes that she too plays a vital role in protecting him from the snare of the enemy. In this way, more than any other, she is truly his God-given "help meet." For his part, he must understand the unusual demands placed upon her as a pastor's wife and do everything he can to strengthen and support her. In this mutual concern they will discover not only each other but love.

Their marriage did not suddenly fail; that is, adultery was not the problem as much as it was the consequence, the end result of several "little" things which were wrong in their relationship. Now they must give these "little foxes" their undivided attention. If these seemingly innocuous issues are not rectified, then their marriage is doomed to mediocrity and possibly another episode of adultery.

Many of these "little" issues are dealt with in the first three chapters of this book, especially Chapters 2 and 3, so I will not deal with them in depth here. Do let me remind you of one, and may this one serve as a model for resolving the others. This one, which plagues almost all ministerial marriages, is "busyness"!

To illustrate the tragic potential this has for the minister's marriage, I quoted (in Chapter 2) Walter Wangerin, Jr., author and pastor, who wrote autobiographically of his own dilemma:

". . . I was ministering. I was a whole human, active in an honorable job, receiving the love of a grateful congregation, charging out the door in the mornings, collapsing in bed at night. I was healthy in society; she was dying in a little house — and accusing herself for the evil of wanting more time from me, stealing the time from God. I laughed happily at potlucks. She cried in secret . . . . In those days the smile died in her face. The high laughter turned dusty in her throat. Privately the woman withered — and I did not see it."[11]

Saying he was sorry wasn't enough, nor was knowing what was wrong and where the fault lay. In order for his marriage to be healed, he had to repent; that is, he had to change the way he managed his life, his marriage and his ministry. Thankfully, he dealt with these issues before his marriage was rent by infidelity. But for the minister who hasn't, it is still not too late. Right now, as God is restoring his marriage, he can make the behavioral changes which will ensure a healthy relationship in the years ahead. Let Wangerin's action serve as a model. He writes:

127

"I said, 'We need to be together.' I meant that with all my heart. And I continued, 'We need to make the time to be together. What I should do,' I said — but would this insult Thanne? — 'What I should do is make appointments on my calendar for you. Oh, forgive me for sounding so businesslike. But I should write it in my schedule book.'

"I said, 'Every night we'll spend the hour before supper together. I'll be home and we'll talk together. I'll write that in my book. What do you think? That doesn't demean you, does it? Maybe it does. But I'll do it.' I said all this to the ceiling. And I said. 'We'll spend a weekend together, you and me alone. Two nights, three days, away from home. Count on it. This year, next year, all the years. I'll be with you. I promise you I will.'

"...In the days that followed, I came home before dinner. A full hour before dinner. And I sat on a stool in the kitchen while Thanne cooked. And this is how I felt: artificial. The little talk we made was mostly forced, and Thanne was mostly silent. Well, our lives had been different in the last years, more divergent than we realized; we had little in common after all. Worse, Thanne was simply not sure whether she could trust my care for her or my change. It would be a risky thing to reveal herself to the one who had hurt her and could hurt her yet again. She did love me. She had rediscovered it and told me so. But I don't think we were friends much.

"The cup, the daily hour, continued empty for a while.

"But even if it was empty, it was *there*. First it had to be that form — and then it might, when the time was right, be filled.

128

"I kept coming home. Even when we didn't talk, I came. It was simple labor, the keeping of a covenant for its own sake, because it had been promised; there is no excitement in this part of the story.

"But the mere persistence of the cup caused Thanne to begin to trust it. If I was there yesterday, then I could be there tomorrow — therefore, she might risk a word or two today. And she did. Thanne began to talk. She began to believe that I would listen. And I did. The more she talked, the more I *wanted* to listen, and the more my own talk wasn't merely self-centered.

"It is a wonder when your beloved trusts you enough to give herself to you again, trusts you with her weight, her treasure, and her life. In time the cup, which had proven itself, began to fill with the serious liquid of our lives. What a valuable vessel is a cup, a covenant!

"Now, though we may be separate in the morning, the ideas that occur to us apart we save for the hour when we will be together, because we trust in that hour; and it is as though we'd been together the whole day through. If Thanne suffers another sin of mine, it needn't swell in secret until it explodes. The cup is there for it, a place for it, and I drink from the cup, both the medicine that wakens and purges me, and the love with which she nourishes me."[12]

The key for him was an act of his will. He recognized what was wrong and *decided* to do something about it. Change of this nature is never easy; in fact, it often feels forced, artificial. Don't despair! In time these changes will bear fruit. For now they are like seeds planted in the ground of your relationship. There must be a period of germination, followed by a time of growing, before you are finally ready to reap the harvest. In fact, his faithfulness during this "artificial" time will do a great deal to restore her trust, and, as her trust grows, she will dare to risk loving him again.

Adultery is, indeed, a deadly blow to any marriage, but especially to a minister's marriage with all of the accompanying fall-out. Still, it need not be the end. With God's help, competent Christian counseling, and a determined commitment on the part of both spouses, their marriage can be healed and restored. In fact, their renewed relationship can be far better than the old marriage, for they have now eliminated many of the issues which contributed to the adultery, thus improving their marriage significantly.

Truly God can take the very worst the enemy brings upon us and use it for our eternal good. Not that He wills it (the adultery), a thousand times no! But He can redeem it; that is, use it to contribute to our ultimate Christlikeness.

Footnotes

[1]Walter Wangerin, Jr., *As For Me And My House* (Nashville: Thomas Nelson, Inc., 1987), pp. 206,207.

[2]Florence Littauer, *Lives On The Mend* (Waco: Word Books Publisher, 1985), p. 86.

[3]Heather Bryce (a pen name), "After the Affair: A Wife's Story," *Leadership* (Winter Quarter, 1988), p. 60.

[4]Ibid, p. 64.

[5]Wangerin, pp. 199,200.

[6]Dr. Richard D. Dobbins, "Saints in Crisis," *Grow* (Akron: Emerge Ministries, Vol. 13, Issue 1, 1984), p. 8.

[7]Desmond Morris, *Intimate Behavior* (New York: Random House, 1971), pp. 73-78.

[8]James Dobson, *Love Must Be Tough* (Waco: Word Books Publisher, 1983), p. 196.

[9]Ibid, p. 198.

[10]H. Norman Wright, *Communciation: Key to Your Marriage* (Ventura: Regal Books, 1974), p. 164.

[11]Wangerin, p. 87.

[12]Ibid, pp. 109,110.

Chapter 7

RESHAPING

THE MINISTRY

As I approach this final chapter, I keep asking myself the question: "Can immorality in the ministry be prevented?" The most honest answer is no; that is, not completely. The issues involved are too complex, the attack of the enemy too subtle and unrelenting, and the personalities of the men and women in the ministry simply too varied to realistically think that all ministerial immorality can be eliminated.

Having said that, let me hasten to add that I do think that we can significantly reduce the number of incidents, but to do so we will have to reshape the way we do ministry. By that I mean, we will have to re-examine and adjust the way we prepare people for ministry. We must establish new models: servant leaders, rather than charismatic personalities. We must help the minister set new goals for himself and his ministry: spiritual character goals, rather than personal power.

Our standards of ministerial success can no longer be borrowed from the world system. We may claim that bigger is not necessarily better, but in reality a minister's influence is usually in direct proportion to the size of the church he pastors. And the vast majority of leadership positions go to men who have succeeded in the numbers game — baptisms, budgets, and buildings.

Finally, we must address the crying need ministers have for in-depth relationships with one another.

Preparing the Minister for the Ministry

Dr. Gary R. Collins, professor of psychology at Trinity Evangelical Divinity School, writes: "Gordon Allport, past president of the American Psychological Association and a professor at Harvard, once said the biggest problem with pastors in this country is that they have no interpersonal skills. That's a harsh statement, I realize, but he's not completely wrong. Pastors, if they are not careful, can relate to books and theological ideas far better than they relate to people."[1]

He goes on to say: "A former student of mine recently said, 'One characteristic of many Yuppies is that they are very good at managing their careers but not the other parts of their lives.' I think pastors are like that sometimes. They are better at managing the church than managing their families, their bodies, their time, or their spiritual lives. *And we didn't prepare them in seminary. The only thing we taught them to manage was the Hebrew text.*"[2] (emphasis mine)

Perhaps our educational model is flawed, patterned too much after the university structure. The minister cannot be prepared to do ministry the way a person is trained to be an engineer or an accountant. He needs more than an intellectual grasp of scripture, theology, and church history; more than an overview of church administration. The ministry is an expression of who the minister is more than what he knows; it flows out of his character, his spirit, not from his intellect. In most other professions it is what a man knows that prepares him for his task. In the ministry it is *Who he knows* (Christ) and his personal relationship with Him.

Almost all Bible colleges pay lip service to this concept — and, sincerely, I might add. But that's as far as it goes, at least formally. Consider the core curriculum: courses in English, history, science and philosophy that we may produce ministers with a well-rounded education. Courses in Bible and hermeneutics so they can interpret the scriptures. Courses in theology and homiletics so they can preach well. Courses in psychology so they can learn to counsel, in music so they can lead worship should the need arise, and even courses in physical education so they can be physically fit. But in the typical Bible college curriculum there is not a single course for credit on the devotional life, or intercessory prayer, or fasting. Typically, seminaries are equally lacking in this area.

These, I have heard it argued, are personal spiritual disciplines and therefore need not be included in the required courses. Personal, indeed, but that does not mean that they should be excluded from the core curriculum. When we award credits for courses in church music, but not for the devotional life, we are making a statement about our values, about what we consider important preparation for the ministry. The message the ministerial student receives is that directing worship is more important, to his effectiveness in ministry, than his spiritual life.

With the increased emphasis on the intellectual side of ministerial training, we are producing, not spiritual men and women, not ministers, but academicians.

In addition to some basic changes in the core curriculum, the Church must also consider a change in the way courses are taught. Our institutions of higher learning must return to a vocational approach to ministerial training rather than adhering to the more academic one which has been assumed in recent years.

For instance, a course on the devotional life could include both a survey of the devotional disciplines, practiced by men of God throughout Church history, as well as a "lab" in which the various disciplines are actually practiced. The emphasis would be on "doing" rather than simply "learning about." This same type of format could also be utilized for courses on intercessory prayer, fasting, and signs and wonders. Something not unlike the course that John Wimber taught at Fuller Theological Seminary for a number of years.

The men and women we graduate from our Bible colleges and seminaries must be spiritually mature persons who are well grounded in personal spiritual discipline. They must also have a *working* knowledge of ministry, a knowledge which simply cannot be gained apart from participation in actual ministry. Perhaps ministerial candidates should be required to do a one-year (full-time) internship before they can graduate, certainly before they can be ordained.

In short, we must be about the business of training people to *be* and *do*, not just to know.

The scriptural model for ministerial training, in both the Old and New Testament, is the discipleship model. In the Old Testament, it was called "the school of the prophets" and referred to a group of prophets-in-training who actually lived and ministered with the prophet. They learned through instruction, demonstration, and participation. Jesus used this same model with His own disciples. For three years He literally poured His life into them. He taught them publicly and personally. They witnessed His ministry, and they ministered with Him. They prayed together, ate together, and lived together. The early Church continued this same practice. Barnabas trained John Mark, as did the Apostle Peter. Paul trained young Timothy and a number of others.

The discipleship model is especially effective because it is built on relationship and accountability. No one can read Paul's letters to the churches without realizing the depth of relationship he had with his co-workers, his disciples. They shared his life and ministry even as they prepared for ministry on their own. In addition, they learned ministry first-hand, by doing it with and under the guidance of the apostle himself.

In a recent *Leadership* interview Chuck Swindoll said: "A couple of years ago I attended my first meeting of the board of Dallas Seminary. I was a rookie, and surrounding this table were all these wise, responsible people. But I risked expressing my concern: 'We just graduated two hundred and some people last night. I see their grade-point average, and I'm impressed. Can anybody speak for the character of any of these graduates?'

"There was a long pause.

"I continued, 'I don't have any particular student in mind. In fact, I'd probably endorse them just on the basis of your recommendation. But can anybody here say these graduates have "the goods"?'

"Now I have great respect for what this and many other seminaries are doing. But what concerned me is that ministry is a character profession. You can sleep around and still be a skillful brain surgeon. But you can't do that in ministry without its coming back and seriously impacting your ministry."[3]

Now that is one of the strengths of the discipleship model. It is built on relationship and gives the mentor opportunity to develop the disciple's character as well as his intellect. Some will undoubtedly argue that while the discipleship model is, indeed, scriptural, and undoubtedly effective, it just isn't very practical for our age. The logistical difficulties alone, they will contend, are imposing, if not impossible. Still, if we are serious about stemming the tide of ethical shabbiness and moral indiscretions which are now tainting the ministry, we must be willing to take radical steps.

Modifying our system of ministerial training is just one such step. It will be both time-consuming and costly, not to mention controversial. In the end, however, the benefits to both the minister, and the churches he serves, will more than justify the effort. It is my prayer that those who are in a position to address these issues may catch the vision and flesh it out. The very effectiveness of the ministry may well depend on it.

New Models for Ministry

With the advent of television, and the development of satellite communications in the last twenty years, more and more emphasis has been placed on talent in the ministry. In order to compete with the secular media, and its bigger-than-life renditions, many ministers have developed an entertainment-type format for ministry. Through the use of television and radio, many of them have been able to do enormous good for the Kingdom, while developing a national identity of their own. Since we have already addressed the special temptations which accompany such a vast ministry (Chapter 4), I will not reiterate them here. Instead, let us consider the impact this situation has had on the average minister.

At one time the most esteemed ministers were men of impeccable character. They had staying power, or as one man said, they "wore well." The better you knew them, the more you respected them. The power of their ministry was in their faithfulness, their integrity, their willingness to serve. They literally poured out their lives in ministry with little thought of personal recognition. Their highest reward was the approval of God, and the trust and respect of their congregation.

The books produced by this earlier generation of ministers give evidence to the things they held dear. *My Utmost For His Highest* by Oswald Chambers, *The Necessity of Prayer* by E. M. Bounds, *A Serious Call to a Devout and Holy Life* by William Law, *The Pursuit of God* by A. W. Tozer, *With Christ in the School of Prayer* by Andrew Murray, to name just a few.

In many cases, these models for ministry have been replaced by the more visible radio and television ministers of our day. I do not mean to categorically imply that these ministers are not worthy models, only that what we see on television is a one-dimensional presentation of the ministry,

139

an incomplete picture at best — and that one dimension becomes our model. Where is the minister who visits the hospital, calls on the elderly, counsels the troubled, marries the young and buries the dead? Where is the man of God who mingles with his flock, who builds relationships that last a lifetime, who serves as an example of Christian service to the whole congregation? The servant leader is gone, replaced by a charismatic personality.

At least unconsciously, many ministers have replaced their call to serve with a call to success. This is both a personal problem and a corporate one. It is personal in the sense that each minister is responsible to guard his own heart. He must root out worldly ambition and fleshly pride with a sanctified ruthlessness. Corporately, it is the Church's responsibility to continually model servant leadership and true humility. We must never promote a minister who is not a worthy model, for those we promote, through recognition and highly visible ministry opportunities, will inevitably become our models. If we constantly reward those who are talented and successful, while overlooking their obvious shortcomings, we are, in a none too subtle way, communicating a message which says that success is more important than character.

Let me hasten to add that a minister can be talented, successful (I like the term *effective* better), and a true model of servant leadership as well.

As we think about appropriate models for ministry, let me direct your attention to our spiritual roots:

"Brothers, think of what you were when you were called. Not many of you were wise by human standards; not many were influential; not many were of noble birth. But God chose the foolish things of the world to shame the wise; God chose the weak things of the world to shame the strong. He chose the lowly things of this world and the despised things — and the things that are not — to nullify the things that are, so that no one may boast before him. It is because of him that you are in Christ Jesus, who has become for us wisdom from God — that is, our righteousness, holiness and redemption. Therefore, as it is written: "Let him who boasts boast in the Lord.' "

1 Corinthians 1:26-31

New Goals for the Minister

By our very nature we human beings are goal-orientated and, as a result, we often build our self-esteem on our achievements. Ministers are no exception. Unfortunately, our efforts can seldom be measured by an objective standard. Or as David Seamands says: "We pastors really don't have a way to know whether we are successes or failures. We're trying to please a lot of people, and sometimes we don't please any."[4] As a result we are often tempted to set material goals rather than spiritual ones. For instance, we sometimes measure our success by the size of our congregation, the kind of car we drive, the salary we make, the positions we hold in our denomination or even the number of outside invitations we receive.

Such an attitude, though common, is deadly. It turns colleagues into competitors. We are constantly measuring our "success" against our neighbor's. If our accomplishments exceed his, we are tempted to pride. If they don't, we flirt with despair and jealousy.

I once found myself trapped in that vicious cycle. I couldn't compete. In a system in which a minister's value is measured by the numbers — baptisms, budget and buildings — I was simply outclassed. For the first fourteen years of ministry, I pastored small churches (under 100 members) in remote rural areas. For years I focused on accomplishment, and experienced an unending cycle of frustration. No matter how much I accomplished there was always more to do, another mountain to climb, another problem to solve. In addition, I was always looking up to see some minister whizzing by in the fast lane. His achievements dwarfed mine, made them seem despairingly insignificant.

In desperation, I took my sagging self-esteem to God. In His presence I began to discover a new way of determining my self-worth. Instead of the numbers game, over which I had only the slightest control, I realized I could base my success on my relationship with Him. I set new goals — character goals, spiritual goals. I measured myself, not by the numbers, nor against the achievements of other ministers, but by my potential Christlikeness.

I discovered that the highest goal of ministry is not "doing" but *"becoming."* God has predestined us, not to success, but to Christlikeness. Paul writes, "For those God foreknew he also predestined to be conformed to the likeness of his Son..." (Rom. 8:29).

There was still the work of the ministry to be done, but now it was the by-product of my relationship with the Lord, an expression of who I was in Him, rather than an attempt to prove my worth. And I found myself focusing on character and Christlikeness, rather than any material standard of success. It wasn't power I sought, but purity; not the acclaim of men, but the favor of God. The more fully I was able to appropriate this truth, the more liberated I became. I was content, rather than competitive; able for the first time to genuinely rejoice in the achievements of my peers.

The blessings of such an attitude are truly manifold. While pastoring small churches, in difficult areas, I was free from the doubt and depression which is often so much a part of the ministry when "success" is measured by achievements rather than by spiritual character. Now that I've experienced a measure of "success," this attitude protects me from pride. Any time I start to feel pretty smug about the size of "my" church, or the books "I" have published, God reminds me of our covenant. He seems to say, "Richard, if you couldn't build your self-worth on the size of your congregation when it numbered less than 100 people, you can't do it now that it numbers more than a 1000."

Don't misunderstand me, such an attitude isn't easy, and it certainly doesn't come naturally. I must constantly battle against spiritual pride and competitiveness. Over and over, continually it seems, I must submit myself to the sanctifying work of the Spirit. Still, I don't think I could experience anything like the freedom I've known if God hadn't enabled me to exchange my personal power goals for the character goals He has for my life.

Imagine, if you will, the potential for genuine fellowship that exists in the Kingdom of God where the greatest is the servant of all, where each and every one prefers all others above himself, and where pleasing Jesus is our only ambition. The possibilities of such a fellowship are almost beyond me; yet in my heart of hearts, it's what I long for: to be like Him, and to be one with you.

New Measurements for Ministry

As we develop new goals we must also adopt an objective standard for measuring the authenticity of our

143

ministry. Interestingly enough, the major emphasis of scripture is on the minister rather than the ministry. When Jesus warns His listeners about false prophets, He tells them to examine their character, not their ministry:

" 'Watch out for false prophets. They come to you in sheep's clothing, but inwardly they are ferocious wolves. *By their fruit you will recognize them.* Do people pick grapes from thornbushes, or figs from thistles? Likewise every good tree bears good fruit, but a bad tree bears bad fruit . . . .

" 'Not everyone who says to me, "Lord, Lord," will enter the kingdom of heaven, but only he who does the will of my Father who is in heaven. Many will say to me on that day, "Lord, Lord, did we not prophesy in your name, and in your name drive out demons and perform many miracles?" Then I will tell them plainly, "I never knew you. Away from me you evildoers!" ' " (emphasis mine)

Matthew 7:15-17,21-23

Notice that false prophets appear authentic enough: "They come to you in sheep's clothing . . ." (that is, they look the part, talk the part; they may even preach effectively and work miracles) ". . . but inwardly they are ferocious wolves." (v. 15) The only way to discern them is by their character, the fruit of their lives, not the results of their ministry.

By contrast, the world system measures "success" by the "bottom line," the end result. A man's character has little bearing on his standing in the community as long as he sins discreetly and continues to make a profit. This is an unfortunate commentary on our times, but it is doubly tragic when the Church uses a religious version of the "bottom line" to determine success in the ministry.

In a recent *Christianity Today* interview, Richard Dortch is quoted: "Sometimes I think the church doesn't know anything about true success. It's all tied to how many stations we have on our network, or how big our building is. It's so easy to lose control, to compromise without recognizing it. At PTL, there was no time taken for prayer or for family, because the show had to go on. We were so caught up in God's work that we forgot about God. It took the tragedy, the kick in the teeth, to bring us to our senses."[5]

I have a friend, something of a country preacher, who puts this warning in his own unforgettable vernacular. He says, "Watch out for the prophets who are after the gold, the glory, or the girls." Richard Foster calls it money, sex, and power. Either way, I think, it is a pretty fair interpretation of what Jesus was talking about. When we measure our ministry, we must not look at the outward trappings, but at our heart, our motives! We must learn to ask ourselves hard questions and then to answer them with a fearless honesty.

Am I greedy? Am I in the ministry for personal gain?

Paul warns about ministers who ". . . have been robbed of the truth and who think that godliness is a means to financial gain" (1 Tim. 6:5). He says:

". . . Some people, eager for money, have wandered from the faith and pierced themselves with many griefs.

"But you, man of God, flee from all this, and pursue righteousness, godliness, faith, love, endurance and gentleness."

1 Timothy 6:10,11

145

Am I ambitious? Do I seek recognition and acclaim? Am I a proud man, a power broker?

Pride and ambition often go hand in hand in the minister's life. They often manifest themselves in the most subtle fashion. Eugene Peterson, pastor of Christ Our King Presbyterian Church in Bel Air, Maryland, relates a personal experience which illustrates this danger well:

". . . during our recent building project, we had a financial goal, and we passed it. Everybody was elated. But I was furious, because I felt they had set the goal too low in the first place. I thought people had held back and been stingy.

"I got on my prophetic horse and wrote a letter to the congregation that said, 'You are stingy,' almost that blunt. Before I sent it, I told the Session, 'I've prayed about this,' (that usually gets them on your side) 'and I feel strongly about needing to say this,' and read the letter to them.

"Silence.

"One man said, 'Don't send that.' Another man said, 'I'm disappointed that you would do that.' Voice by voice they told me not to send it.

"I went home that night mad at the Session. Jan said, 'Could it be they were listening to God more than you were?' It hadn't occurred to me.

"A week later I knew they were right, dead right. That wasn't righteous, prophetic indignation. That was just my ego ticked because I thought I had a congregation in the palm of my hand, and they didn't do what I wanted."[6]

Even as I type that, I can see myself. In fact, what minister can't? We get used to having our own way and then we get mad when something doesn't go the way we planned. Unless we deal with that attitude, and quickly, we may disqualify ourselves for ministry, for the scripture says: "An elder must be blameless . . . . not overbearing, not quick-tempered . . . not violent" (Titus 1:6,7). "Do nothing out of selfish ambition or vain conceit, but in humility consider others better than yourselves" (Phil. 2:3).

Am I morally pure, or is there some hidden seed of lust in me?

Paul says: ". . . among you there must not be even a hint of sexual immorality, or of any kind of impurity, or of greed, because these are improper for God's holy people. Nor should there be obscenity, foolish talk or coarse joking, which are out of place . . . . For of this you can be sure: No immoral, impure or greedy person . . . has any inheritance in the kingdom of Christ and of God" (Eph. 5:3-5).

Am I emotionally whole? Am I spiritually mature?

Writing to the young minister Timothy, Paul exhorts him:

"Don't let anyone look down on you . . . but set an example for the believers in speech, in life, in love, in faith and in purity . . . .

"Be diligent in these matters; give yourself wholly to them, so that everyone may see your progress. Watch your life and doctrine closely. Persevere in them . . . ."

1 Timothy 4:12,15,16

Our new measurement of ministry is based on character, not accomplishment, thereby freeing us from the pressures of the world system. Our only goal is inner purity, personal obedience and faithfulness to God and His word. Our only standard for success is inward and spiritual: ". . . to be made new in the attitude of . . . (our) . . . minds; and to put on the new self, created to be like God in true righteousness and holiness" (Eph. 4:23,24).

"In other words," writes Bruce Shelley, professor of church history at Denver Seminary, "the ministry (is) more than communicating a religious message; it (is) a life commending the grace and holiness of God."[7]

New Relationships in the Ministry

If we are, indeed, serious about protecting ourselves from the perils of power, then we will accept the responsibility for building relationships in which we are known intimately and held accountable.

For the pastor this may assume a variety of forms — with his session, his elders, or his board. Generally, he is accountable to them for the work of the ministry, his conduct in the course of his ministerial duties. Additionally, he will need a circle of peers, usually no more than four or five, with whom he can develop a relationship of mutual accountability. When he strays, they can correct him; when he grows weary, they can strengthen and encourage him; when he becomes confused, they can provide guidance; and when he celebrates, they can celebrate with him!

Corporately, the Church must reconsider the way it provides spiritual care for its ministers. In many cases, no one, it seems, is directly responsible for their spiritual oversight and well-being. Several different district officials are responsible in part, but, as is often the case, when many share a mutual responsibility, then no one really sees that it gets done. The critical nature of this current crisis demands that we re-examine our priorities and re-budget our resources, if necessary. Whatever the cost, we must provide better and more personal spiritual care for our ministers. Their eternal destiny may well depend on it.

I'm reminded of the story of the Scottish sheepherder who missed Sunday services for several weeks in a row. Finally his pastor went to visit him. As fate would have it, the day was blustery and cold and the sheepherder was sitting in his tiny hut before a small fire. He invited the pastor to join him and they sat in silence for several minutes. Then the pastor got up, and taking the tongs, he removed a burning coal from the fire and placed in on the hearth. In just a matter of minutes it was smoking and then it grew gray and cold. After a bit he got up and returned it to the fire where it promptly burst into flames. He then excused himself and without a word returned home. The old sheepherder got the message and the next week he was back in service.

We really do need each other, don't we?

Without question, the Body of Christ has suffered injury. Highly visible spokesmen of national stature have fallen prey to the perils of power. As I write this, Jim and Tammy Bakker are in seclusion in the California desert. Jimmy Swaggart has left the Assemblies of God and plans to return to his pulpit in just a few weeks. Many other lesser known ministers and their wives are also struggling to put the pieces of their lives and their ministries back together. Individually and collectively it is tragic, yet even in this moment of shame I am hopeful. If we can learn from our mistakes this too may prove to be a redemptive experience in the life of the Church. The God we serve has a history of redeeming life's rejects and restoring them.

"I thank Christ Jesus our Lord, who has given me strength, that he considered me faithful, appointing me to his service. Even though I was once a blasphemer and a persecutor and a violent man, I was shown mercy because I acted in ignorance and unbelief. The grace of our Lord was poured out on me abundantly, along with the faith and love that are in Christ Jesus.

"Here is a trustworthy saying that deserves full acceptance: Christ Jesus came into the world to save sinners — of whom I am the worst. But for that very reason I was shown mercy so that in me, the worst of sinners, Christ Jesus might display his unlimited patience as an example for those who would believe on him and receive eternal life. Now to the King eternal, immortal, invisible, the only God, be honor and glory for ever and ever. Amen."

1 Timothy 1:12-17

Footnotes

[1]Dean Merrill, *Clergy Couples in Crisis* (Waco: Word Books Publisher, 1985), p. 26.

[2]Ibid, p. 25.

[3]"How Pure Must a Pastor Be?" *Leadership* (Spring Quarter, 1988), p. 13.

[4]"Private Sins of Public Ministry," *Leadership* (Winter Quarter, 1988), p. 20.

[5]"I Made Mistakes," *Christianity Today* (Mar. 18, 1988), p. 47.

[6]"How Pure Must a Pastor Be?" p. 19.

[7]Bruce Shelley, "The Character Question," *Leadership* (Spring Quarter, 1988), p. 32.

BIBLIOGRAPHY

Alcorn, Randy. "Strategies To Keep From Falling." *Leadership*, Winter Quarter, 1988.

"A Talk with the MacDonalds," *Christianity Today*, 10 July, 1987.

"A Year to Forget," *Christianity Today*, 18 March, 1988.

Benson, Bob, and Benson, Michael W. *Disciplines for the Inner Life*. Waco: Word Books, 1985.

Broderick, Carlfred. *Couples*. New York: Simon and Schuster, 1979.

Bryce, Heather (a pen name). "After the Affair: A Wife's Story." *Leadership*, Winter Quarter, 1988.

Christianity Today, 18 March, 1988.

Christianity Today, 10 July, 1987.

Claypool, John. *Stages: The Art of Living the Expected*. Waco: Word Books, 1977.

Cole, K.C. "Playing Together: From Couples That Play." *Psychology Today*, February 1982.

Dobbins, Richard D. "Saints in Crisis." *Grow*. Akron: Emerge Ministries, Inc., Volume 13, Issue 1, 1984.

Dobson, James. *Love Must Be Tough.* Waco: Word Books, 1983.

Exley, Richard. *Blue-Collar Christianity.* Tulsa: Honor Books, A Division of Harrison House, 1988.

Exley, Richard. *The Rhythm of Life.* Tulsa: Honor Books, A Division of Harrison House, 1987.

Fee, Gordon D. "The First Epistle To The Corinthians." *The New International Commentary On The New Testament.* Grand Rapids: William B. Eerdmans, 1987.

Foster, Richard J. *Money, Sex & Power.* San Francisco: Harper & Row, 1985.

"Good News for the Disenfranchised," *Christianity Today,* 18 March, 1988.

Guinn, G. Earl. "The Resurrection of Jesus." *The Twentieth-Century Pulpit.* Nashville: Abingdon, 1978.

"How Common Is Pastoral Indiscretion?" *Leadership,* Winter Quarter, 1988.

"How Pure Must a Pastor Be?" *Leadership,* Spring Quarter, 1988.

"I Made Mistakes," *Christianity Today,* 18 March, 1988.

Kreitler, Peter, with Bruns, Bill. *Affair Prevention.* New York: MacMillan, 1981.

Kushner, Harold. *When All You've Ever Wanted Isn't Enough.* New York: Summit Books: A Division of Simon & Schuster, Inc., 1986.

Littauer, Florence. *Lives On The Mend.* Waco: Word Books, 1985.

Merrill, Dean. *Clergy Couples in Crisis.* Waco: Word Books, 1985.

Morris, Desmond. *Intimate Behavior.* New York: Random House, 1971.

Name Withheld. "The War Within: An Anatomy of Lust." *Leadership,* Fall Quarter, 1982.

"Private Sins of Public Ministry," *Leadership,* Winter Quarter, 1988.

Schaefer, Tom. "Sex and the Clergy." *Wichita Eagle Beacon,* 5 March, 1988.

Shelley, Bruce. "The Character Question." *Leadership,* Spring Quarter, 1988.

Swaggart, Jimmy. "The Lord Of Breaking Through." *The Evangelist.* March 1988.

"The Fall of Jimmy Swaggart," *People Weekly,* 7 March, 1988.

U.S. News & World Report, 25 October, 1983.

Wangerin, Walter, Jr. *As For Me And My House.* Nashville: Thomas Nelson, 1987.

Wright, H. Norman. *Communication: Key to Your Marriage.* Ventura: Regal Books, 1974.

Wright, H. Norman. *Seasons of a Marriage.* Ventura: Regal Books, 1982.